DEVOTIONS

Inspired by the *FRESH START BIBLE*

DIRECTION FOR EVERY DAY

Devotions Inspired by the *Fresh Start Bible*
Copyright © 2019 by Gateway Church

Written by *Robert Morris, Jen Weaver, Hannah Etsebeth, Tom Lane, Elizabeth Settle, Al Pearson, Mary Jo Pierce, David Blease, Aaron Wronko, Chelsea Seaton, Todd Lane, Kyle Fox, Thomas Miller, Bridgette Morris, Zach Neese, Derek Dunn, Jade Washington, Sion Alford, Monica Bates, Tim Sheppard*

Editorial Director *Shea Tellefsen*
Senior Editor *Daniel Hopkins*
Contributing Editor *Stacy Burnett*
Copy Editor *Georgette Shuler*
Project Coordinator *Alena Moore*

Creative Director *Solomon Ross*
Art Director *Tim Lautensack*
Designer *Perri Adcock*
Designer *Emanuel Puşcaş*
Print Coordinator *David Phillips*

Requests for information should be addressed to:
Gateway Publishing®, 500 S Nolen, Southlake, TX 76092
licensing@gatewaypeople.com

Fresh Start Bible One-Year Reading Plan taken from the *Fresh Start Bible,* © 2019 Gateway Press®. Used by permission. All rights reserved.

All Scripture citations are taken from the *Holy Bible, New Living Translation,* Copyright © 1996, 2004, 2015, by Tyndale House Foundation. Used by permission of Tyndale House Publishers, Inc., Carol Stream, Illinois 60188. All rights reserved.

Some names and details of actual events have been changed to protect the identities of the persons involved.

All rights reserved. No portion of this publication may be reproduced, stored in a retrieval system, or transmitted in any form by any means—electronic, mechanical, photocopying, recording, or any other—except for brief quotations in printed reviews, without the prior permission of the publisher.

The *Fresh Start Bible* is available for purchase at freshstartbible.com.

Printed in the United States of America.

ISBN 978-1-951227-26-5

CONTENTS

Preface 7

Day 01 God's Greatest Desire *By Robert Morris* 11

Day 02 A Conversation *By Jen Weaver* 15

Day 03 Flooded *By Hannah Etsebeth* 19

Day 04 God's Assignment *By Tom Lane* 23

Day 05 God's Promise to You *By Elizabeth Settle* 27

Day 06 The Reward of Obedience *By Al Pearson* 31

Day 07 God's Intentional Interruption *By Mary Jo Pierce* 35

Day 08 A Good Eye *By David Blease* 39

Day 09 Keep Knocking *By Aaron Wronko* 43

Day 10	"I Am Willing" *By Chelsea Seaton*	47
Day 11	You Want Me to Do What? *By Todd Lane*	51
Day 12	Dive In *By Kyle Fox*	55
Day 13	Your Birthright *By Thomas Miller*	59
Day 14	Let Me Handle This *By Bridgette Morris*	63
Day 15	Muzzling Monsters *By Zach Neese*	67
Day 16	What Is Your Name? *By Derek Dunn*	71
Day 17	Nourished and Restored *By Jade Washington*	75
Day 18	On the Outside Looking In *By Sion Alford*	79
Day 19	It Starts with the Heart *By Monica Bates*	83
Day 20	The Leaven of Heaven *By Tim Sheppard*	87
Day 21	Your Destiny Will Come *By Robert Morris*	91
	Fresh Start Bible One-Year Reading Plan	95
	The 15-Minute Breakthrough *By Robert Morris*	117
	Memory Verses	123

PREFACE

Did you know God wrote the Bible for *you*? He inspired 40 different writers to compose 66 books over 1,500 years, and He did it for *you*. God gave us His Word to breathe life into us, fill us with His love, and light our paths.

That's why I'm especially excited about this year's devotional! In fact, it's more than just a devotional; it's the start of your journey to reading through the Bible. It leads you into the *Fresh Start Bible* reading plan, which will guide you through the entire Bible in a year. The Scriptures are in the New Living Translation, which puts the thought of each verse into more contemporary language for easier understanding. While this devotional focuses on the first 21 days of the reading plan—it's just the beginning! Three weeks from now, you'll be well on your way to reading the entire Bible in a year.

As you read this devotional, it's my prayer that you'll receive a renewed passion and hunger for God's Word. I hope that once you finish these 21 days, you'll have created a habit of reading the Bible every day and listening for what the Holy Spirit says. In fact, the key to change and growth is hearing, believing, and obeying what God says to you through His Word. My hope is that you wake up each day excited to see what God will speak to you through His Word.

If you commit to making this devotional and the *Fresh Start Bible* reading plan part of your daily routine over the next year, I promise you'll never be the same. God can and will change your life!

Robert Morris

Pastor Robert Morris

DAY 1

TODAY'S READING PLAN

Genesis 1-2
+
Psalm 1
+
Proverbs 1:1-7
+
Matthew 1

GOD'S GREATEST DESIRE

By Robert Morris

Then God said, "Let us make human beings in our image, … . "
Genesis 1:26

Have you ever wondered why you were created? The answer can be found by looking at Adam, the first person God created.

Adam lived in the Garden of Eden and spent time with God every day, yet he had a desire for something more. One day when Adam was with God, I imagine he said, "God, I love *everything* in the garden! I enjoy walking with You and talking with You, but I'm lonely. I have a longing for something more."

While that conversation isn't in the Bible, Genesis 2:20 does say, "[Adam] gave names to all the livestock, all the birds of the sky, and all the wild animals. But still there was no helper just right for him."

So what did God do? "The Lord God caused the man to fall into a deep sleep. While the man slept, the Lord God took out one of the man's ribs and closed up the opening. Then the Lord God made a woman from the rib, and he brought her to the man" (Genesis 2:21- 22).

How did God know the *only* thing that would satisfy the desire of Adam's heart was a bride? It's because He has the same desire. God desires a bride, and the bride is *you*! So that longing Adam had for something more? It was *for* God and *from* God! Scripture says God has placed eternity within the hearts of man (see Ecclesiastes 3:11)—not so it would drive us crazy but so it would drive us closer to Him!

You were created to love God, but it's your choice. You see, God created you in His image, which means He created you with a will because He has a will. He chose to create you, His bride, in hopes that you would love Him as much as He loves you.

God's greatest desire is *you* and that you would choose to love Him. Will you make that choice today?

PRAYER

God, thank You for creating me in Your image and giving me free will to choose how I will live my life. Today, I choose to live for You and to love You. Thank You for putting a desire for You in my heart. In Jesus' name, Amen.

HOLY SPIRIT, WHAT ARE YOU SAYING TO ME TODAY?

DAY 2

TODAY'S READING PLAN

Genesis 3–4
+
Psalm 2:1-6
+
Proverbs 1:8-9
+
Matthew 2

A CONVERSATION

By Jen Weaver

When the cool evening breezes were blowing, the man and his wife heard the Lord God walking about in the garden. So they hid from the Lord God among the trees. Then the Lord God called to the man, "Where are you?" *Genesis 3:8–9*

"Where are you?"

All-knowing God called out to the man He'd crafted with His own fingertips, asking a question yet already knowing the answer. I've often pictured God in this moment as a chuckling parent, standing behind Adam and pretending not to see him. But when reading this passage again, I gained a different perspective.

In an instant, Adam learned of his vulnerable condition and faced shame followed by fear. He assumed that his disobedience ruined everything, and all the good times were over forever. So when he heard God walking nearby, Adam didn't dare run into the presence of his Creator; he hid, ashamed and afraid.

God chose not to peel back trees with a breath, revealing Adam's hiding spot. He didn't march through the garden broadcasting the serpent's cunning words or send angels to evict them without getting personally involved. Instead, God affirmed

His desire for relationship by inviting Adam into a conversation.

"Where are you?"

He didn't start with questions about what they had done, who they had spoken to, how they had disobeyed, or whose fault it was. No, God started with the question closest to His heart. Father God created us to be near, and Adam had hidden himself away.

"Adam, I love you, I'm eager to spend time together, and you've placed yourself apart from Me. Where are you?"

I imagine Adam evaluating his situation, crouched there in his patch of trees. *Where am I? You know I'm here. You probably see me even though I'm trying to avoid you. I'm right here.*

> In the Garden of Eden. Slouched behind these flimsy branches. Cloaked in shame. Frozen in fear. Distancing myself from You.

Then Adam made the best decision he'd made all day. Above the noise of his failure and beyond the shouts of shame and fear, He listened to God's voice calling for him. And he replied.

PRAYER

Lord, thank You for creating me to be near to You. No matter how many times I make the wrong choice, You still want me to be close. Today I choose to draw close to You. In Jesus' name, Amen.

HOLY SPIRIT, WHAT ARE YOU SAYING TO ME TODAY?

DAY

3

TODAY'S READING PLAN

Genesis 5-6
+
Psalm 2:7-12
+
Proverbs 1:10-19
+
Matthew 3

FLOODED

By Hannah Etsebeth

"But I will confirm my covenant with you. So, enter the boat—you and your wife and your sons and their wives"… So Noah did everything exactly as God had commanded him. *Genesis 6:18, 22*

It was an age of spiritual darkness on the earth, and it didn't make any sense. Foretelling a massive flood. Building a boat. Filling it with animals. Proclaiming he heard from God. But Noah knew what he had heard, and he pressed on. He built the boat. He endured the ridicule. He gathered the animals. He looked to heaven and trusted God.

Then the earth *flooded*.

Surrounded by the cackle of the chicken, the lowing of the cattle, the roar of the lion, and the sound of rain … for 40 days. There was no end in sight. I wonder if Noah's inner dialogue sounded something like, *Will the waters recede? Will I see land again? Did I hear Him right? Can God be trusted?*

In the end, a dove returned with a fresh olive leaf, proving the waters receded. God's covenant was made complete. Sound familiar? We read the promise. We hear it. It resonates in our spirit, and we lean into it. But over time as we wait for the waters to recede, doubt enters.

Will the waters recede? Will I see land again? Did I hear Him right? Can God be trusted?

Generations have lived to tell the story of the Great Flood. Not because of the water, but because of the promise it carried. God's word can be trusted. And that promise is emphasized every time we cast our eyes on a rainbow coloring the sky with its splendor.

Perhaps today you hear His quiet whisper, reassuring your soul:

"The waters in your life will recede. *I'll show you the way.*

"You will see land again. *Lean into my word.*

"I can be trusted."

PRAYER

God, today I choose to trust in You. I believe that Your word is true, and Your promises last a lifetime. Thank You for being a light unto my path. In Jesus' name, Amen.

HOLY SPIRIT, WHAT ARE YOU SAYING T

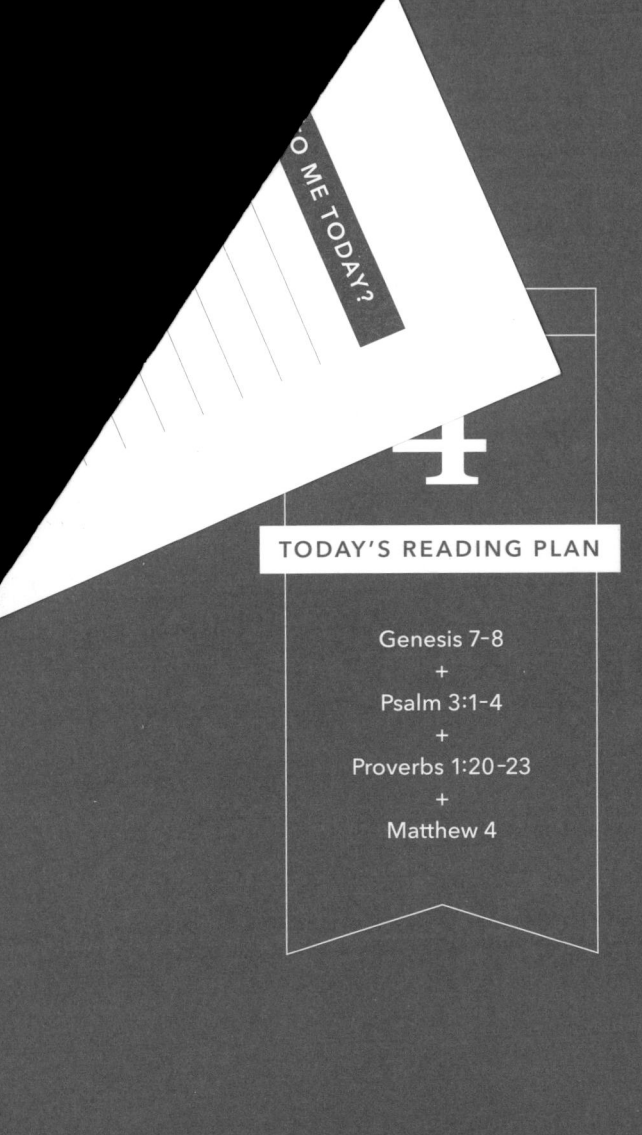

4

TODAY'S READING PLAN

Genesis 7–8
+
Psalm 3:1-4
+
Proverbs 1:20-23
+
Matthew 4

GOD'S ASSIGNMENT

By Tom Lane

Then Noah built an altar to the Lord, and there he sacrificed burnt offerings the animals and birds that had been approved for that purpose. And the Lord was pleased with the aroma of the sacrifice and said to himself, "I will never again curse the ground because of the human race .... I will never again destroy all living things." *Genesis 8:20–21*

Can you imagine how Noah felt when God told him all humanity was going to be destroyed and he was to build an ark? Genesis 6:8 tells us that Noah was a righteous man, blameless in his generation, and had found favor in the eyes of the Lord.

Even then, I think it was overwhelming for him to hear God's command to build a ship that was 450-feet long, 75-feet wide, and 45-feet tall. After all, it had never rained on the earth, and there was no vast body of water nearby. Noah didn't have an engineering degree or any ship-building experience. The only thing he had was a command from God. It is estimated that it took Noah between 55 and 75 years to build the ark.

PRAYER

...ank You for the assignment ...iven me. I choose to believe ...Your commands in my life. ... at how You work things ...ver and over again, and ...ill do that in my life. In ...en.

...on.
...ed for his
... year while the
...vered and recovering
...the flood, and he witnessed the miraculous power of God firsthand.

When we say yes to God's command and walk with Him in our assignment, we get to experience revelation, see His mighty work, experience the orchestration of events to fulfill the work, live under God's grace of protection and provision, and witness His miraculous power firsthand.

Has God given you an overwhelming assignment? Will you follow Noah's example and experience God's work in a mighty and powerful way in your life?

HOLY SPIRIT, WHAT ARE YOU SAYING TO ME TODAY?

DAY 5

TODAY'S READING PLAN

Genesis 9–10
+
Psalm 3:5-8
+
Proverbs 1:24-27
+
Matthew 5:1-26

GOD'S PROMISE TO YOU

By Elizabeth Settle

I lay down and slept, yet I woke up in safety, for the Lord was watching over me. *Psalm 3:5*

As you read through today's Scriptures, do you notice an intermingling of God's blessings and earthly disappointments?

In Genesis 9:1, God blesses Noah, and his family gets a new start. However, that blessing contrasts what happens later in Genesis 9:22-25. Noah is shamed by his youngest son, and he puts a curse on his own grandson, Canaan.

Here's another instance. In Psalm 3:5, David acknowledges God's protection, "I lay down and slept, yet I woke up in safety, for the Lord was watching over me." Amidst the disappointments of family battles and sad situations, David tapped into the powerful reality that he slept in safety because God was alert to his plight, and He hadn't abandoned His promise to protect him.

Finally, in one of the most provocative combinations of blessing and disappointment, there are The Beatitudes in which Jesus proclaims paradoxical blessings in verse after verse of Matthew 5. Blessed are the *poor*, the *sad*, the *lowly* and *needy*, the *understated,* and *kind* for "theirs is the kingdom of heaven."

Today we continue to experience earthly disappointments, but as in every age, Scripture reminds us that God is alert to our plight, and He has not abandoned His blessings and promise to us. That promise is that God is with us.

What do today's readings say to you?

You might be experiencing family battles and difficult situations. You might be struggling with sadness and anxiety. Will you trust that the Lord is watching over you? He knows your plight and is faithful to fulfill His promise to you—even if you feel bound by shame, grief, conflict, or injustice.

PRAYER

Lord, I choose to stop and become aware of Your faithful covering. Will You give me ears to hear what You are saying and eyes to see how You are protecting me? Thank you for watching over me. In Jesus' name, Amen.

HOLY SPIRIT, WHAT ARE YOU SAYING TO ME TODAY?

DAY

6

TODAY'S READING PLAN

Genesis 11-12
+
Psalm 4:1-5
+
Proverbs 1:28-33
+
Matthew 5:27-48

THE REWARD OF OBEDIENCE

By Al Pearson

The Lord had said to Abram, "Leave your native country, your relatives, and your father's family, and go to the land that I will show you. I will make you into a great nation. I will bless you and make you famous, and you will be a blessing to others. I will bless those who bless you and curse those who treat you with contempt. All the families on earth will be blessed through you." So Abram departed as the Lord had instructed, ... *Genesis 12:1–4*

Growing up, I heard many stories about Abraham, his travels, the victory of rescuing his nephew, and his submission to the word of God regarding his son Isaac. I even sang a song written about Abraham and his "many sons." However, rarely did I hear about the sacrifice Abraham made to follow an unfamiliar God to be obedient.

Imagine for a moment this guy who is a heathen hears the voice of God telling him to leave his country, his relatives, and his own family to go to a foreign land he knew nothing about? This is a picture of "blind obedience" that I know all too well.

Back in 2004, there was a business opportunity that compelled me to leave everything I'd known for 30 years and move to a place I'd never even visited. The thought of my wife leaving her close-knit family as well as me leaving the *only* place I'd developed deep roots was difficult and scary. The sacrifice was going to be great for my wife, our twins, and me. However, we trusted God and chose to follow His leading.

In hindsight, we can see that God was preparing us for something much bigger than we would have experienced had we resisted His voice prompting us to move.

Too often our flesh is tempted to enjoy the comfort of the familiar and the ease of the known; however, obedience requires sacrifice. Obedience is not just *about* you, nor is its reward just *for* you. Sacrificial obedience also provides a blessing for those walking with you and after you. Abraham's obedience led to becoming the father of many nations, which led to the greatest reward—the birth of Jesus. And through Jesus' obedience, we are now called the "children of God" (Romans 8:14-15).

Maybe today God is reminding you of a step you need to take or a change you need to make. Are you willing to sacrifice the cost of comfort for the reward of obedience?

Remember, "God causes everything to work together for the good to those who love God…" (Romans 8:28) even though at times it may not feel good. Just trust that the reward of obedience is always worth it!

PRAYER

Lord, today I choose to obey You. I know You have a plan for me, and though it may not look like my plan, I believe Your plan is best. Lead me today. In Jesus' name, Amen.

HOLY SPIRIT, WHAT ARE YOU SAYING TO ME TODAY?

DAY 7

TODAY'S READING PLAN

Genesis 13-14
+
Psalm 4:6-8
+
Proverbs 2:1-5
+
Matthew 6:1-18

GOD'S INTENTIONAL INTERRUPTION

By Mary Jo Pierce

So Abram left Egypt and traveled north into the Negev, along with his wife and Lot and all that they owned. "I am giving you this land, as far as you can see, to you and your descendants as a permanent possession."... There he built another altar to the Lord. *Genesis 13:1, 15, 18b*

Well into what my husband and I imagined retirement to be, God interrupted our lives. He used circumstances beyond our control to move us to another state. Unlike Abraham I did not go willingly. I just couldn't imagine why God would take us from our family, friends, home, church, and ministry. It felt lonely. It felt confusing. It felt *final*.

Only in hindsight do I see the sovereign, loving, *I-know-the-plans-I-have-for-you* God who has directed our steps. He was writing the most rewarding, significant chapter of our lives, and we didn't even realize it. We chose to view that season as a test that we were intent on passing. A test of trusting, waiting, praying, and fasting. A test of giving thanks "in all circumstances."

And then suddenly, as quickly as God had moved us to another state, He brought us back home and opened doors we could not have imagined. We were beginning to see the fruit of that season of testing and trusting.

- Ruth didn't know she was destined to be the great grandmother of King David and in the legacy line of our King Jesus.

- Moses didn't know when God said, "Now go, for I am sending you to Pharaoh. You must lead my people Israel out of Egypt," that it would involve a nation's destiny.

- Mary didn't know when she said, "I am the Lord's servant. May everything you have said about me come true," that God had planned to come to earth in the form of a baby as the promised Messiah.

- The Apostles didn't know when Jesus said, "Come. Follow Me," that 2,000 years later, people would still be responding to that same call.

Do you know? It takes courage, faith, and time to trust God when He interrupts your plans for His. If we will simply follow Him in what He tells us today, the blessing will be our descendants.

PRAYER

God, thank You for Your divine interruptions. I'm sorry for getting frustrated when my plans get in the way of Yours. Today I will submit my plans to You, and I pray that Your will be done in my life. In Jesus' name, Amen.

HOLY SPIRIT, WHAT ARE YOU SAYING TO ME TODAY?

DAY

8

TODAY'S READING PLAN

Genesis 15-16
+
Psalm 5:1-6
+
Proverbs 2:6-8
+
Matthew 6:19-34

A GOOD EYE

By David Blease

"Your eye is like a lamp that provides light for your body. When your eye is healthy, your whole body is filled with light. But when your eye is unhealthy, your whole body is filled with darkness. And if the light you think you have is actually darkness, how deep that darkness is!" Matthew 6:22–23

When reading the Bible, we often forget that we are reading the words of people from 2,000 years ago in a different place and culture. When we do this, Scripture can lose some of its nuance and meaning. I never understood what Jesus was saying in Matthew 6, so for years I did what most people do—*I skipped it*.

But when I learned about the Jewish culture and viewed Jesus as a Jewish rabbi, my eyes were opened to so many Scriptures I had misinterpreted because I didn't understand the Jewish culture.

In Jesus' day there was a Hebraic idiom that was used to describe a person's outlook toward others. The idiom was to have a "healthy eye," or more literally, a "good eye."

Having a "good eye" meant you looked at others with compassion and had a generous spirit. A person with the "evil eye" or "unhealthy eye" is one without compassion and greedy for money. This expression is still used in Israel today. When people go through Jerusalem raising money, you may hear them say, "Please give with a good eye!" The same idiom is found in Proverbs 22:9: "A generous man [literally, 'a good eye'] will be blessed, for he shares his food with the poor."

When our eye is good, Jesus says our body will be full of light. How could it not be? Looking compassionately at others and being generous—it sounds like the light of Jesus to me! And vice versa, having a "bad eye" means we are filled with darkness, unable to show the light of Jesus due to our greed and lack of compassion. It means holding on tightly to what we have, resenting those with more, and refusing to help those with less.

When you are generous, you not only show compassion and generosity for others (just like Jesus did) but you also communicate the trust you have in God that He will provide for you! Let us show the light of Christ today, let us have a good eye, showing compassion and generosity toward others. Shine bright and love big!

PRAYER

Lord, thank You for Your provision in my life. I know You will take care of me, and today I choose to be generous just as You have been generous with me. In Jesus' name, Amen.

HOLY SPIRIT, WHAT ARE YOU SAYING TO ME TODAY?

DAY

9

TODAY'S READING PLAN

Genesis 17-18
+
Psalm 5:7-12
+
Proverbs 2:9-22
+
Matthew 7

KEEP KNOCKING

By Aaron Wronko

"Keep on asking, and you will receive what you ask for. Keep on seeking, and you will find. Keep on knocking, and the door will be opened to you. For everyone who asks, receives. Everyone who seeks, finds. And to everyone who knocks, the door will be opened." *Matthew 7:7-8*

Have you ever asked God for something and when the answer didn't come right away, you decided to figure it out on your own? Take a look at today's reading plan. God promised Abraham a son. But when the promise took longer than expected, Abraham and Sarah decided to take matters into their own hands and Ishmael was born. When we do what Abraham and Sarah did, it causes us to stop *asking* and *seeking* God. Why ask God in faith and why seek Him when we've come up with our own solution?

When we live a lifestyle of asking, seeking, and knocking, we are consistently coming before God. In Matthew 6:33, Jesus tells us to "Seek the kingdom of God above all else." This isn't something we just do once. Seeking—*praying*—is how we set our compass. Prayer is how we live. The God of the universe has extended to us an invitation to continually ask, seek, and knock.

It was 13 years before God came back to Abraham to talk about the promised son that Sarah was destined to birth. Isaac was a son of faith, in the same way God wants us to walk by faith. After all, it takes faith to continue asking, seeking, and knocking.

There are times in life when we feel confident to pray and to seek God. But there are also times when we hit roadblocks. We feel discouraged. The wind has been taken out of our sails, and we don't see the answer we're looking for. What do we do in those times? We keep on asking and seeking. We do this because when we communicate with our Father, it's an ongoing dialogue. God loves the relationship; He loves the conversation; and He loves to see you walk in faith.

What are you believing God for? What have you been seeking God about? What doors are you asking Him to open? Keep on asking. Keep on seeking. Keep on knocking.

PRAYER

God, I'm so grateful that I can have an ongoing conversation with You. Thank You for allowing me to come to You with my struggles. I will put my trust in You and continue seeking You in every area of my life. In Jesus' name, Amen.

HOLY SPIRIT, WHAT ARE YOU SAYING TO ME TODAY?

DAY 10

TODAY'S READING PLAN

Genesis 19-20
+
Psalm 6:1-5
+
Proverbs 3:1-4
+
Matthew 8:1-17

"I AM WILLING"

By Chelsea Seaton

Suddenly, a man with leprosy approached him and knelt before him. "Lord," the man said, "if you are willing, you can heal me and make me clean." Jesus reached out and touched him. "I am willing," he said, "Be healed!" And instantly the leprosy disappeared. *Matthew 8:2–3*

Leprosy isn't a disease we hear about anymore, but in Jesus' time it was a common and terrible sickness. If you touched someone with leprosy you would contract the disease. Not only did people with the disease have to cover themselves, but they had to yell, "Unclean!" so everyone would know not to come near them. They had to isolate themselves to live with others who had the same disease. It was often thought if you had leprosy it was because of some sin you had committed, and God was punishing you. I cannot imagine the shame these people carried around believing they had to be isolated because of sin they had in their past. Actually— I *can imagine it.*

When I sin, shame is quick to whisper "Unclean" and make me feel like I'm the worst person of all time. It tells me I'm a super sinner. A fraud.

There's no way I should work at a church, and am I even a Christian? Ok the last question may be extreme. But it's true! Sin and shame go hand in hand and make us feel like modern-day lepers in a hopeless situation. But shame is a liar.

Satan uses shame to tell you that you're too far gone—that like the leper you need to isolate yourself and hide under the cloth of regret so no one sees, and if a healthy person tries to get close, you need to run the other direction back with the other unclean people.

But you are never too far gone from Jesus' reach. This Scripture in Matthew shows us that when we come to Him and ask for His healing touch, He is quick to reach out His hand. Jesus is not afraid of your past, and you are never too far gone from His presence. He is waiting to instantly heal every hopeless situation.

Wherever you are today, whatever you're dealing with, you can ask Jesus to come and heal that situation. He is waiting, He is ready, and He is willing.

PRAYER

Lord, thank You for redeeming every area of my life. Even when I have sinned and feel distant from you, Your presence is near and You are quick to heal. Today, I will bring my struggles to You. In Jesus' name, Amen.

HOLY SPIRIT, WHAT ARE YOU SAYING TO ME TODAY?

DAY 11

TODAY'S READING PLAN

Genesis 21-22
+
Psalm 6:6-10
+
Proverbs 3:5-6
+
Matthew 8:18-34

YOU WANT ME TO DO WHAT?

By Todd Lane

"Take your son, your only son—yes, Isaac, whom you love so much—and go to the land of Moriah. Go and sacrifice him as a burnt offering on one of the mountains, which I will show you."
Genesis 22:2

As a husband and a father, I can imagine several obstacles for me if I were Abraham taking Isaac up on the mountain to sacrifice him. Among those would be having to tell my wife what God told me to do! I can imagine why verse 3 says, "The next morning Abraham got up *early.*" I think he was trying to sneak out without telling Sarah!

I wonder if between verses 2 and 3, Abraham thought, *You want me to do what?* I mean, who wouldn't have that thought? Isaac was the answer to their prayers. And Isaac was the promise from God for their legacy. In the previous chapter (Genesis 21:12), Abraham had sent away Hagar and Ishmael because God said "... for Isaac is the son through whom your descendants will be counted." Abraham had gone all in. There were no other options that he could see for the fulfillment of God's promise. He must have been so confused. And there he found himself facing the ultimate test: to simply trust God.

Proverbs 3:5 says, "Trust in the Lord with all your heart; do not depend on your own understanding." Every disciple who is developing an intimate relationship with God will have opportunities to obey God in ways that will require us to abandon our own understanding and trust Him at a whole new level. But it's almost like God gets great joy in showing *His* supernatural provision when *we* sacrificially trust and obey.

When God provided a ram to sacrifice instead of Isaac, that was when God revealed Himself as Jehovah Jireh, meaning the Lord will provide. But that provision only arrived once Abraham proceeded with sacrificial obedience. It's as if God reveals this aspect of Himself in the most critical moment when we find ourselves clinging to His word alone. Then suddenly, out of nowhere, the Lord provides in a way we couldn't have imagined.

When we find ourselves asking God, "You want me to do what?" perhaps He is saying back to us, "Watch how I will provide."

PRAYER

God, I will trust You with your calling and assignment for me. I believe in Your provision in my life, and I will choose to cling to Your word even when things look impossible. In Jesus' name, Amen.

HOLY SPIRIT, WHAT ARE YOU SAYING TO ME TODAY?

DAY 12

TODAY'S READING PLAN

Genesis 23-24
+
Psalm 7:1-5
+
Proverbs 3:7-8
+
Matthew 9:1-17

DIVE IN

By Kyle Fox

The servant watched her in silence, wondering whether or not the Lord had given him success in his mission. *Genesis 24:21*

Is this too good to be true?! Is it this easy? Is this the person I am supposed to approach? If I had been in Abraham's servant's shoes searching for Isaac's wife, I would have asked the Lord many of these questions. But he had prayed for God to make his mission successful, and verse 15 tells us that he saw Rebekah approaching the well for water before he'd even finished praying.

His assignment and the answer to his prayer was right in front of him, but doubt was almost his deterrent. How much time do I waste wondering, like the servant, whether or not I have heard the Lord?

Have you ever asked the Lord for opportunities to reach people, then wondered whether or not you're supposed to start a conversation with the person directly in front of you? I have. Sometimes ministry is simpler than we make it out to be. What if that nudge you feel to approach someone is the result of someone else praying for that person, paired with you asking the Lord for opportunities? What if the distance between a person and their breakthrough is the distance between you and that person? What if in that moment, God chose you to reach them?

Abraham's servant could have assumed Rebekah was at the well by chance. It's easy to assume those around us at church, work, or school end up in our proximity by coincidence, but assumption is the enemy of connection.

When presented with an opportunity, we have choices: doubt or dive in. Stay silent or speak up. Shrink back or step out. The same God who places the person in front of you is faithful to put the courage to act inside of you. And He will make your mission successful.

PRAYER

Lord, thank You that You've put me on a mission to reach people. Give me boldness and confidence to speak to those around me and share Your love with them. In Jesus' name, Amen.

HOLY SPIRIT, WHAT ARE YOU SAYING TO ME TODAY?

DAY

13

TODAY'S READING PLAN

Genesis 25-26
+
Psalm 7:6-9
+
Proverbs 3:9-10
+
Matthew 9:18-38

YOUR BIRTHRIGHT

By Thomas Miller

"Look, I'm dying of starvation!" said Esau. "What good is my birthright to me now?" *Genesis 25:32*

After a long, hot day in the wilderness, Esau was tired. In fact, he was exhausted. And to make matters that much worse, he was hungry. Simply put, Esau was completely depleted. Being fatigued and famished, he made a decision that would affect the rest of his life. In that moment, Esau chose to give all of his birthright to his younger brother in exchange for a temporary fix: some bread and stew.

In Biblical times, the birthright of the firstborn son had to do with his long-term position and inheritance. As the firstborn, Esau was to become the leader of the family and receive a double portion of the overall inheritance from his father. Yet in a moment of impulsive reasoning, Esau gave it all away. He chose to fix his temporary pain instead of standing on a permanent promise.

In moments of physical and emotional exhaustion, we are at our most vulnerable. It is in these moments that the enemy comes to tempt us with different "solutions" to fix our fatigue. Sometimes the pain in those moments feels so insurmountable, any solution seems better than no solution. Just like Esau showed contempt for his birthright (Genesis 25:34), the enemy wants us to fully disregard our birthright and to make a hasty decision outside of God's perfect plan for our lives.

In those moments, we must stand on God's permanent promises and remember our birthright. We must remember our position and our inheritance. We are God's children, and no one can take us from Him (John 10:28-29); we are seated with Him right now in the heavenly realms (Ephesians 2:6); heaven is our inheritance (1 Peter 1:4); God is our defender (Psalm 7:9); and His power works within us and helps us in our weaknesses (Romans 6:11; 8:11, 26-28). All that plus all the promises in God's Word make up our inherited birthright as children of God!

What a wonderful birthright! And it's all yours.

PRAYER

Father, thank You for the birthright You've given me. I am Your child and I have a great inheritance from You. Give me endurance and persistence in my walk with You so that when the enemy comes to steal it, I will hold onto Your truth. Thank You for Your promises. In Jesus' name, Amen.

HOLY SPIRIT, WHAT ARE YOU SAYING TO ME TODAY?

DAY

14

TODAY'S READING PLAN

Genesis 27-28
+
Psalm 7:10-17
+
Proverbs 3:11-12
+
Matthew 10:1-15

LET ME HANDLE THIS

By Bridgette Morris

God is my shield, saving those whose hearts are true and right.
Psalm 7:10

Have you ever been wronged? Maybe someone talked badly about you behind your back. Maybe someone cheated you or stole from you. How are we as Christians supposed to respond?

The Bible tells us in this Scripture: keep your heart true and right, and God will be your shield.

It sounds simple but walking it out can be tricky. A few years back a friend told me that someone had said something hurtful about me to a number of people. I had a choice to defend myself or let God deal with the person and my reputation. I prayed about it and decided to let God be my shield in the situation and not pursue fixing anything on my own.

I ended up never hearing anything else from that person, and what they said basically fell flat. After that situation, I actually had favor in the area I was slandered. I know that was the Lord's favor due to me keeping my heart right. People will hurt us, and the Lord will redeem us if we keep our hearts right.

Think about it, God didn't say to keep your *words* right. You can easily grit your teeth and say, "Bless your heart." Keeping your *heart* right, the place that only the Lord can see, is a true representation of your spiritual maturity. Keeping your heart right can only come from confidence and an understanding of God's love, will, and control.

If God's going to be our shield we have to stay out of His way and let *Him* work it out.

A few years ago, my son Parker found red paint in a closet of our house and spilled some of it on the carpet. He tried to "clean it up," only rubbing it into the carpet and walls. If my sweet son had just come to me as soon as it happened and let me clean it up, it wouldn't have made such a mess. God can clean up our messes much better than we can. He promises to be our shield if we keep our hearts right and true.

PRAYER

God, thank You for being my shield. Help me to keep my heart right and true even when I'm faced with difficult situations. I believe that You are my redeemer and protector, and I will continue to trust in You. In Jesus' name, Amen.

HOLY SPIRIT, WHAT ARE YOU SAYING TO ME TODAY?

DAY 15

TODAY'S READING PLAN

Genesis 29-30
+
Psalm 8:1-2
+
Proverbs 3:13-18
+
Matthew 10:16-42

MUZZLING MONSTERS

By Zach Neese

You have taught children and infants to tell of your strength, silencing your enemies and all who oppose you. *Psalm 8:2*

There's a word for telling of God's strength: *praise*. When my son was little he would often wake from nightmares in a trembling, sweat-sheened panic. "Son," I would tell him, "whenever fear comes against you, praise Jesus and it has to go away. Jesus is bigger and stronger than any man, monster, or demon. And they are scared of Him." I would pray with him and remind him that the Lord doesn't give him a spirit of fear but of power, love, and self-discipline (2 Timothy 1:7). It takes self-discipline for a little boy to trust God's love and strength when he's afraid. I can't tell you how many nights I heard his sweet little voice from down the hallway singing, "Jesus loves me, this I know…" as he learned to war against his monsters. The simplest of songs, the strongest of truths, is a muzzle over the lying lips of the enemy.

Someday I am sure we will stand in awe at the legions that have been mobilized to the tunes of children's songs.

As adults, our greatest enemy is not some creepy-crawly beneath our beds. Instead, our enemy appears in whispered accusations, lurking anxieties, and nagging doubts. Our enemy is that false prophet of our tomorrows: *fear*. Fear is not just an emotion. According to 2 Timothy 1:7, it is a spirit. Fear is our enemy accusing God of being too weak to help us and too distant to care.

Those are lies.

Just as Satan lied to Eve in the garden, he lies to us as we toss and turn in our beds at night. It can feel like an unstoppable onslaught, but there is a shield to protect us from a hoard of fear—it's praise. All it takes to make him shut up is your child-like agreement with a simple, irrefutable truth. Jesus *loves me*! God is Good! He is strong and kind, merciful, and mighty to save.

Praise is expressing the truth about God, and truth is the only way to win a war of words with the devil. Just praise, and let the truth of God slap the enemy in the mouth.

PRAYER

Father, today I will praise You, and I'm so grateful that Your praise drives away the spirit of fear and the lies of the enemy. You are good, and You have given me love, power, and sound mind. Thank You, God. In Jesus' name, Amen.

HOLY SPIRIT, WHAT ARE YOU SAYING TO ME TODAY?

DAY 16

TODAY'S READING PLAN

Genesis 31–32
+
Psalm 8:3-9
+
Proverbs 3:19-20
+
Matthew 11

WHAT IS YOUR NAME?

By Derek Dunn

"What is your name?" the man asked. He replied, "Jacob." "Your name will no longer be Jacob," the man told him. "From now on you will be called Israel, because you have fought with God and with men and have won." *Genesis 32:27–28*

In the ancient Near East, your name was more than just a word your parents called you. Your name was how others viewed you. It was a look into your soul, a reflection of your choices, a snapshot of your character; it was your identity.

Today, while your name is special, it most likely doesn't fully describe who you are. However, what you call yourself is still very important to God. In fact, your name as a follower of Christ is, "Child of God." This name describes how God sees you—your true identity.

God wants you to know *who* you are, and He wants you to know how He views you. He knows if you will embrace what *He* thinks about you, then it will shape what *you* think about you, and what *you* think about you will shape the way you live.

But how many times have your thoughts about *you* been shaped by your past, mistakes, failures, hurts, words people have spoken about you, or lies you've believed? This was Jacob's reality.

If you're hearing a name spoken over your life that is something other than, "Child of God," then God wants to change that, but it will come with a wrestle. Only after wrestling did Jacob receive his new name, Israel—his true identity.

God invites you to wrestle with all the other names spoken over you. Instead of running from your past, mistakes, failures, hurts, words people have spoken over you, or lies you've believed, He brings you face to face with those names. As you present all these to God, He will say, "No longer will that be your name." He will speak your true name and identity to you. You're safe with Him. He knows who you really are. He will call you by your true name.

PRAYER

Lord, thank You that my true identity is found in You. You have wiped away every lie that the enemy has spoken to me and made me a child of God. Thank You for Your safety and protection. In Jesus' name, Amen.

HOLY SPIRIT, WHAT ARE YOU SAYING TO ME TODAY?

DAY

17

TODAY'S READING PLAN

Genesis 33–34
+
Psalm 9:1-6
+
Proverbs 3:21-26
+
Matthew 12:1-21

NOURISHED AND RESTORED

By Jade Washington

And He answered, "If you had a sheep that fell into a well on the Sabbath, wouldn't you work to pull it out? Of course you would. And how much more valuable is a person than a sheep! Yes, the law permits a person to do good on the Sabbath." Then He said to the man, "Hold out your hand." So the man held out his hand, and it was restored just like the other one! Then the Pharisees called a meeting to plot how to kill Jesus." *Matthew 12:11–14*

As the Pharisees were plotting to kill Jesus, He was leading His disciples through a grain field where they plucked the heads of grain from the stalks because they were hungry. However, it was the Sabbath, and the Pharisees took issue with it. "Look, your disciples are breaking the law by harvesting grain on the Sabbath" (Matthew 12:2).

Later in the same chapter, Jesus went into the synagogue and saw a man with a withered hand. The Pharisees asked Him if it was lawful to heal on the Sabbath. Of course, Jesus healed the man saying, "It is lawful to do good on the Sabbath."

He had allowed His disciples to be nourished by grain, and He healed the broken.

The Pharisees led from a place of jealousy and arrogance, but Jesus led from a place of authority and compassion. He saw people as children—not competition. More importantly though, what we see in Matthew 12 is that the Pharisees valued the law and works, but Jesus valued people. And that's what He's teaching us.

When we grow closer to Him, we begin to see as He sees. Our compassion for others grows, and we begin to value others even more. As we are nourished in Him, we see the hungry and the weary. As we are restored in Him, we see the broken and ashamed. As we rest in Him, we are strengthened to lift up those who are down.

In today's passage of Scripture, Christ reveals the heart of the Father. His compassion changed those around Him. That same freedom and authority is available to us today as we allow ourselves to be nourished and restored by Him.

PRAYER

God, thank You that a love for You leads to a love and compassion for others. Help me to see those around me who are struggling, and help me to be a vessel of Your restoration in their lives. In Jesus' name, Amen.

HOLY SPIRIT, WHAT ARE YOU SAYING TO ME TODAY?

DAY 18

TODAY'S READING PLAN

Genesis 35–36
+
Psalm 9:7-10
+
Proverbs 3:27-30
+
Matthew 12:22-50

ON THE OUTSIDE LOOKING IN

By Sion Alford

As Jesus was speaking to the crowd, his mother and brothers stood outside asking to speak to him. Someone told Jesus, "Your mother and your brothers are standing outside, and they want to speak to you." Jesus asked, "Who is my mother? Who are my brothers?" Then he pointed to his disciples and said, "Look, these are my mother and brothers. Anyone who does the will of my Father in heaven is my brother and sister and mother!"
Matthew 12:46–50

I must admit that when I read the verses above, I was a bit troubled. How could the Son of God have such harsh words for those closest to Him? His mother, Mary, and His brothers must have been shocked at Jesus' response to their request to speak with Him. Imagine it—Jesus was rejecting His family while describing His friends as His true family! It all seems extremely contrary to the nature and character of Jesus. How could this be?

In this story, Jesus used a teaching tool that He used often throughout Scripture to bring light to an important truth. As Matthew 12:46 tells us, Jesus was in the middle of speaking to the crowd when He was interrupted by their request. He turned their request into a sermon illustration and used the comparison as a way to communicate an important truth!

Jesus was not suggesting that we reject our family for the mission of the gospel. He was not commanding us to forget those closest to us so we can pursue our dreams and our calling. He was revealing that our obedience to the will of God is the most important thing we can do as members of God's family! The extent of His comparison should give us clues to the importance of this truth. 1 John 2:5 tells us that "those who obey God's Word truly show how completely they love Him." In other words, when we love God, we can't help but obey Him. Obedience is so important that Jesus once told His disciples, "My nourishment comes from doing the will of God, who sent Me, and from finishing His work." (John 4:34).

Have you ever felt like you were standing on the outside looking in? Has an intimate relationship with God felt like something that others had special privilege to while you struggle with it? Learn from Jesus' words to us that His true family are those who obey the will of the Father. Allow your love for God to lead you to the most important thing you can do—obey His will.

PRAYER

Jesus, thank You for making me a part of Your family. Today I will choose to obey the will of the Father as I draw closer to You. In Jesus' name, Amen.

HOLY SPIRIT, WHAT ARE YOU SAYING TO ME TODAY?

DAY 19

TODAY'S READING PLAN

Genesis 37-38
+
Psalm 9:11-20
+
Proverbs 3:31-35
+
Matthew 13:1-30

IT STARTS WITH THE HEART

By Monica Bates

"But blessed are your eyes, because they see; and your ears, because they hear. I tell you the truth, many prophets and righteous people longed to see what you see, but they didn't see it. And they longed to hear what you hear, but they didn't hear it." *Matthew 13:16–17*

The Lord has blessed my husband and me with three amazing daughters. When I was pregnant with my first daughter, my husband and I set up our first prenatal appointment with the doctor. I was so excited for this visit and had little idea of all that it was going to entail. As they celebrated with us on our pregnancy, the first thing they set out to do was to hear the baby's heartbeat. When we saw the image of our precious child on the ultrasound screen, we listened intently to hear the rhythm of our baby's heart. We did not even think about the child's sex, if the baby had ten fingers and toes or two eyes, ears, legs, and arms. At that moment, we only wanted to hear the rapid cadence through the primitive ultrasound speaker. The Lord whispered to me at that moment, *I care very much about the heart. That is where I start.*

In today's reading plan the authors of Genesis, Psalms, Proverbs, and Matthew share matters of the heart with us. We read about jealousy, impatience, betrayal, trust, and rescue. These are the things that make our hearts beat out of rhythm throughout our lives as we enter into various seasons.

What is the rhythm of your heartbeat with God? Will you allow God to align your heart with His?

PRAYER

Lord, thank You for caring about my heart. I believe that as I draw close to You, You will draw close to me. Help me to hear Your heartbeat. In Jesus' name, Amen.

HOLY SPIRIT, WHAT ARE YOU SAYING TO ME TODAY?

DAY

20

TODAY'S READING PLAN

Genesis 39–40
+
Psalm 10:1-11
+
Proverbs 4:1-6
+
Matthew 13:31-58

THE LEAVEN OF HEAVEN

By Tim Sheppard

"The Kingdom of Heaven is like the yeast a woman used in making bread. Even though she put only a little yeast in three measures of flour, it permeated every part of the dough." *Matthew 13:33*

The word "put" is the Greek word *enkrupto,* from which we get "encryption." It means to hide or conceal (as if by mixing). The woman in the Scripture above kneaded only a little amount of yeast or leaven into 60 pounds of flour. This invisible leaven "permeated every part of the dough," expanding and transforming it in a visible way.

Some expected Jesus to establish an earthly empire. In Luke 17:20-21, the Pharisees, wanting a physical sign, asked Him when the kingdom of God would come. Jesus explained that the kingdom "can't be detected by visible signs." Rather, it is "already among you." Jesus Himself, as leaven kneaded into dough, pervaded society, transforming people's lives.

He is still among us! Through God's redemptive work, the Holy Spirit—the leaven of heaven—is hidden within our hearts. The King and His kingdom permeate every area of our lives, changing us from the inside out!

Inevitably, this invisible kingdom will become visible through us.

Colossians 1:15 says, "Christ is the visible image of the invisible God." Just as God the Father became visible through Jesus, the Holy Spirit "makes us more and more like Him [Jesus] as we are changed into His glorious image" (2 Corinthians 3:18).

Consider Joseph. Jealousy and hatred drove his brothers to sell him into slavery, resulting in Joseph's banishment to Egypt. Even so, God was at work. Despite numerous trials, "the Lord was with Joseph" (Genesis 39:2, 3, 21, 23), and He caused Joseph to succeed in everything he did.

Right now, you may be facing your own battles and asking, "God, why did You allow this to happen?" You can be confident that "God causes everything to work together for the good of those who love God and are called according to His purpose for them" (Romans 8:28). And, just as God used Joseph's exile to restore his family and save a nation from starvation, He just might be hiding you as leaven within the dough of difficulties to allow His kingdom to expand and become visible through you!

PRAYER

Holy Spirit, I pray that You would permeate every part of my life and change me from the inside out. Use me in the situations around me to cause Your kingdom to shine through. In Jesus' name, Amen.

HOLY SPIRIT, WHAT ARE YOU SAYING TO ME TODAY?

DAY

21

TODAY'S READING PLAN

Genesis 41-42
+
Psalm 10:12-18
+
Proverbs 4:7-9
+
Matthew 14:1-21

YOUR DESTINY WILL COME

By Robert Morris

So Pharaoh asked his officials, "Can we find anyone else like this man so obviously filled with the spirit of God?" *Genesis 41:38*

A young man began serving in the church parking lot. Every week he was faithful in that responsibility. After a while his faithfulness became apparent to everyone, and eventually he was made the "parking lot captain." The next week he showed up with a uniform, a bullhorn, and a huge flashlight that looked like a prop from a *Star Wars* movie. He had been given greater power and authority, and that parking lot was now his place of responsibility!

Genesis 41 tells the story of how Joseph stepped into greater power and authority when he was called from the dungeon to interpret Pharaoh's dreams. At that time Joseph had been in prison for 12 years, and it had been 2 full years since he had interpreted the dreams for the butler and the baker. *But things were about to change.*

Not only did Joseph give Pharaoh the interpretation of his dreams, he also told him how to prepare for the coming years of famine (Genesis 41:25-36). Joseph's advice was so full of wisdom it caused Pharaoh to conclude that he must be filled with the Spirit of God.

Pharaoh gave Joseph his signet ring, which represented his rights and authority as the ruler of Egypt. He clothed Joseph in fine linen and put a gold chain around his neck, representing the riches that Joseph would now enjoy. He also had Joseph ride in his chariot, with people crying out, "Bow the knee!" as he went by—which represented the royal position in which Joseph now stood. He had the three *Rs*—rights, riches, and royalty. Now, that's *power!*

Like Joseph, your destiny will come. Stay faithful and don't give up hope! It may be 10, 15, or 20 years—and then, in a single day, God can suddenly change everything about your circumstances! God can bless you and put you into your destiny.

PRAYER

God, I believe that You will fulfill every promise You've made. Even if my circumstances are not how I imagined, I know that You have a great destiny for my life, and I will be faithful and trust in You to complete it. In Jesus' name, Amen.

HOLY SPIRIT, WHAT ARE YOU SAYING TO ME TODAY?

To start this plan on a mobile device, open the YouVersion Bible App and search "Gateway."

FRESH START BIBLE ONE-YEAR READING PLAN

Now that you've completed the first 21 days of the *Fresh Start Bible* One-Year Reading Plan, we encourage you to continue with it the rest of the year!

- **January 1**
  Genesis 1-2
  Psalm 1
  Proverbs 1:1-7
  Matthew 1

- **January 2**
  Genesis 3-4
  Psalm 2:1-6
  Proverbs 1:8-9
  Matthew 2

- **January 3**
  Genesis 5-6
  Psalm 2:7-12
  Proverbs 1:10-19
  Matthew 3

- **January 4**
  Genesis 7-8
  Psalm 3:1-4
  Proverbs 1:20-23
  Matthew 4

- **January 5**
  Genesis 9-10
  Psalm 3:5-8
  Proverbs 1:24-27
  Matthew 5:1-26

- **January 6**
  Genesis 11-12
  Psalm 4:1-5
  Proverbs 1:28-33
  Matthew 5:27-48

- **January 7**
  Genesis 13-14
  Psalm 4:6-8
  Proverbs 2:1-5
  Matthew 6:1-18

- **January 8**
  Genesis 15-16
  Psalm 5:1-6
  Proverbs 2:6-8
  Matthew 6:19-34

- **January 9**
  Genesis 17-18
  Psalm 5:7-12
  Proverbs 2:9-22
  Matthew 7

- **January 10**
  Genesis 19-20
  Psalm 6:1-5
  Proverbs 3:1-4
  Matthew 8:1-17

- **January 11**
  Genesis 21-22
  Psalm 6:6-10
  Proverbs 3:5-6
  Matthew 8:18-34

- **January 12**
  Genesis 23-24
  Psalm 7:1-5
  Proverbs 3:7-8
  Matthew 9:1-17

- **January 13**
  Genesis 25-26
  Psalm 7:6-9
  Proverbs 3:9-10
  Matthew 9:18-38

- **January 14**
  Genesis 27-28
  Psalm 7:10-17
  Proverbs 3:11-12
  Matthew 10:1-15

- **January 15**
  Genesis 29-30
  Psalm 8:1-2
  Proverbs 3:13-18
  Matthew 10:16-42

- **January 16**
  Genesis 31-32
  Psalm 8:3-9
  Proverbs 3:19-20
  Matthew 11

- **January 17**
  Genesis 33-34
  Psalm 9:1-6
  Proverbs 3:21-26
  Matthew 12:1-21

- **January 18**
  Genesis 35-36
  Psalm 9:7-10
  Proverbs 3:27-30
  Matthew 12:22-50

- **January 19**
  Genesis 37-38
  Psalm 9:11-20
  Proverbs 3:31-35
  Matthew 13:1-30

- **January 20**
  Genesis 39-40
  Psalm 10:1-11
  Proverbs 4:1-6
  Matthew 13:31-58

- **January 21**
  Genesis 41-42
  Psalm 10:12-18
  Proverbs 4:7-9
  Matthew 14:1-21

- **January 22**
  Genesis 43-44
  Psalm 11
  Proverbs 4:10-13
  Matthew 14:22-36

- **January 23**
  Genesis 45-46
  Psalm 12
  Proverbs 4:14-17
  Matthew 15:1-20

- **January 24**
  Genesis 47-48
  Psalm 13
  Proverbs 4:18-19
  Matthew 15:21-39

- **January 25**
  Genesis 49-50
  Psalm 14
  Proverbs 4:20-24
  Matthew 16

- **January 26**
  Exodus 1-2
  Psalm 15
  Proverbs 4:25-27
  Matthew 17

- **January 27**
  Exodus 3-4
  Psalm 16:1-6
  Proverbs 5:1-6
  Matthew 18:1-20

- **January 28**
  Exodus 5-6
  Psalm 16:7-11
  Proverbs 5:7-14
  Matthew 18:21-35

- **January 29**
  Exodus 7-8
  Psalm 17:1-5
  Proverbs 5:15-20
  Matthew 19

- **January 30**
  Exodus 9-10
  Psalm 17:6-15
  Proverbs 5:21-23
  Matthew 20:1-16

- **January 31**
  Exodus 11-12
  Psalm 18:1-6
  Proverbs 6:1-5
  Matthew 20:17-34

- **February 1**
  Exodus 13-14
  Psalm 18:7-19
  Proverbs 6:6-11
  Matthew 21:1-22

- **February 2**
  Exodus 15-16
  Psalm 18:20-29
  Proverbs 6:12-15
  Matthew 21:23-46

- **February 3**
  Exodus 17-18
  Psalm 18:30-42
  Proverbs 6:16-19
  Matthew 22:1-22

- **February 4**
  Exodus 19-20
  Psalm 18:43-45
  Proverbs 6:20-25
  Matthew 22:23-46

- **February 5**
  Exodus 21-22
  Psalm 18:46-50
  Proverbs 6:26-29
  Matthew 23:1-22

- **February 6**
  Exodus 23-24
  Psalm 19:1-6
  Proverbs 6:30-31
  Matthew 23:23-39

- **February 7**
  Exodus 25-26
  Psalm 19:7-14
  Proverbs 6:32-35
  Matthew 24:1-35

- **February 8**
  Exodus 27-28
  Psalm 20:1-5
  Proverbs 7:1-5
  Matthew 24:36-51

- **February 9**
  Exodus 29-30
  Psalm 20:6-9
  Proverbs 7:6-23
  Matthew 25:1-30

- **February 10**
  Exodus 31-32
  Psalm 21:1-7
  Proverbs 7:24-27
  Matthew 25:31-46

- **February 11**
  Exodus 33-34
  Psalm 21:8-13
  Proverbs 8:1-5
  Matthew 26:1-25

- **February 12**
  Exodus 35-36
  Psalm 22:1-8
  Proverbs 8:6-11
  Matthew 26:26-56

- **February 13**
  Exodus 37-38
  Psalm 22:9-18
  Proverbs 8:12-21
  Matthew 26:57-75

- **February 14**
  Exodus 39-40
  Psalm 22:19-21
  Proverbs 8:22-31
  Matthew 27:1-31

- **February 15**
  Leviticus 1–2
  Psalm 22:22-31
  Proverbs 8:32-36
  Matthew 27:32-56

- **February 16**
  Leviticus 3–4
  Psalm 23
  Proverbs 9:1-6
  Matthew 27:57-66

- **February 17**
  Leviticus 5–6
  Psalm 24:1-6
  Proverbs 9:7-9
  Matthew 28

- **February 18**
  Leviticus 7–8
  Psalm 24:7-10
  Proverbs 9:10-12
  Mark 1:1-20

- **February 19**
  Leviticus 9–10
  Psalm 25:1-7
  Proverbs 9:13-18
  Mark 1:21-45

- **February 20**
  Leviticus 11–12
  Psalm 25:8-15
  Proverbs 10:1-3
  Mark 2

- **February 21**
  Leviticus 13
  Psalm 25:16-22
  Proverbs 10:4
  Mark 3:1-19

- **February 22**
  Leviticus 14
  Psalm 26:1-5
  Proverbs 10:5-7
  Mark 3:20-35

- **February 23**
  Leviticus 15–16
  Psalm 26:6-12
  Proverbs 10:8
  Mark 4:1-20

- **February 24**
  Leviticus 17–18
  Psalm 27:1-3
  Proverbs 10:9
  Mark 4:21-41

- **February 25**
  Leviticus 19–20
  Psalm 27:4-6
  Proverbs 10:10-12
  Mark 5:1-20

- **February 26**
  Leviticus 21–22
  Psalm 27:7-14
  Proverbs 10:13-16
  Mark 5:21-43

- **February 27**
  Leviticus 23–24
  Psalm 28:1-5
  Proverbs 10:17-18
  Mark 6:1-29

- **February 28**
  Leviticus 25
  Psalm 28:6-9
  Proverbs 10:19-21
  Mark 6:30-56

- **March 1**
  Leviticus 26–27
  Psalm 29:1-9
  Proverbs 10:22-25
  Mark 7:1-23

- **March 2**
  Numbers 1–2
  Psalm 29:10-11
  Proverbs 10:26-29
  Mark 7:24-37

- **March 3**
  Numbers 3–4
  Psalm 30:1-7
  Proverbs 10:30-32
  Mark 8:1-21

- **March 4**
  Numbers 5–6
  Psalm 30:8-12
  Proverbs 11:1-3
  Mark 8:22-38

- **March 5**
  Numbers 7-8
  Psalm 31:1-5
  Proverbs 11:4-6
  Mark 9:1-29

- **March 6**
  Numbers 9-10
  Psalm 31:6-13
  Proverbs 11:7-11
  Mark 9:30-50

- **March 7**
  Numbers 11-12
  Psalm 31:14-18
  Proverbs 11:12-14
  Mark 10:1-31

- **March 8**
  Numbers 13-14
  Psalm 31:19-24
  Proverbs 11:15
  Mark 10:32-52

- **March 9**
  Numbers 15-16
  Psalm 32:1-5
  Proverbs 11:16-18
  Mark 11:1-19

- **March 10**
  Numbers 17-18
  Psalm 32:6-11
  Proverbs 11:19-21
  Mark 11:20-33

- **March 11**
  Numbers 19-20
  Psalm 33:1-5
  Proverbs 11:22-23
  Mark 12:1-27

- **March 12**
  Numbers 21-22
  Psalm 33:6-15
  Proverbs 11:24-26
  Mark 12:28-44

- **March 13**
  Numbers 23-24
  Psalm 33:16-22
  Proverbs 11:27
  Mark 13:1-27

- **March 14**
  Numbers 25-26
  Psalm 34:1-7
  Proverbs 11:28
  Mark 13:28-37

- **March 15**
  Numbers 27-28
  Psalm 34:8-14
  Proverbs 11:29
  Mark 14:1-26

- **March 16**
  Numbers 29-30
  Psalm 34:15-22
  Proverbs 11:30-31
  Mark 14:27-52

- **March 17**
  Numbers 31-32
  Psalm 35:1-10
  Proverbs 12:1
  Mark 14:53-72

- **March 18**
  Numbers 33-34
  Psalm 35:11-16
  Proverbs 12:2
  Mark 15:1-20

- **March 19**
  Numbers 35-36
  Psalm 35:17-28
  Proverbs 12:3
  Mark 15:21-47

- **March 20**
  Deuteronomy 1-2
  Psalm 36:1-4
  Proverbs 12:4-6
  Mark 16

- **March 21**
  Deuteronomy 3-4
  Psalm 36:5-12
  Proverbs 12:7
  Luke 1:1-25

- **March 22**
  Deuteronomy 5-6
  Psalm 37:1-6
  Proverbs 12:8
  Luke 1:26-38

- **March 23**
  Deuteronomy 7-8
  Psalm 37:7-11
  Proverbs 12:9-10
  Luke 1:39-56

- **March 24**
  Deuteronomy 9-10
  Psalm 37:12-15
  Proverbs 12:11
  Luke 1:57-80

- **March 25**
  Deuteronomy 11-12
  Psalm 37:16-22
  Proverbs 12:12-14
  Luke 2:1-24

- **March 26**
  Deuteronomy 13-14
  Psalm 37:23-29
  Proverbs 12:15-16
  Luke 2:25-52

- **March 27**
  Deuteronomy 15-16
  Psalm 37:30-36
  Proverbs 12:17-19
  Luke 3

- **March 28**
  Deuteronomy 17-18
  Psalm 37:37-40
  Proverbs 12:20-22
  Luke 4:1-30

- **March 29**
  Deuteronomy 19-20
  Psalm 38:1-8
  Deuteronomy 12:23-25
  Luke 4:31-44

- **March 30**
  Deuteronomy 21-22
  Psalm 38:9-22
  Proverbs 12:26-28
  Luke 5:1-16

- **March 31**
  Deuteronomy 23-24
  Psalm 39:1-6
  Proverbs 13:1-3
  Luke 5:17-39

- **April 1**
  Deuteronomy 25-26
  Psalm 39:7-11
  Proverbs 13:4-6
  Luke 6:1-26

- **April 2**
  Deuteronomy 27-28
  Psalm 39:12-13
  Proverbs 13:7-8
  Luke 6:27-49

- **April 3**
  Deuteronomy 29-30
  Psalm 40:1-5
  Proverbs 13:9-10
  Luke 7:1-35

- **April 4**
  Deuteronomy 31-32
  Psalm 40:6-10
  Proverbs 13:11-12
  Luke 7:36-50

- **April 5**
  Deuteronomy 33-34
  Psalm 40:11-17
  Proverbs 13:13-14
  Luke 8:1-25

- **April 6**
  Joshua 1-2
  Psalm 41
  Proverbs 13:15-16
  Luke 8:26-56

- **April 7**
  Joshua 3-4
  Psalm 42:1-4
  Proverbs 13:17-18
  Luke 9:1-17

- **April 8**
  Joshua 5-6
  Psalm 42:5-11
  Proverbs 13:19-21
  Luke 9:18-36

- **April 9**
  Joshua 7-8
  Psalm 43
  Proverbs 13:22-23
  Luke 9:37-62

- **April 10**
  Joshua 9–10
  Psalm 44:1-3
  Proverbs 13:24-25
  Luke 10:1-24

- **April 11**
  Joshua 11–12
  Psalm 44:4-19
  Proverbs 14:1-2
  Luke 10:25-42

- **April 12**
  Joshua 13–14
  Psalm 44:20-26
  Proverbs 14:3
  Luke 11:1-28

- **April 13**
  Joshua 15–16
  Psalm 45:1-9
  Proverbs 14:4-5
  Luke 11:29-54

- **April 14**
  Joshua 17–18
  Psalm 45:10-17
  Proverbs 14:6
  Luke 12:1-31

- **April 15**
  Joshua 19–20
  Psalm 46:1-6
  Proverbs 14:7-11
  Luke 12:32-59

- **April 16**
  Joshua 21–22
  Psalm 46:7-11
  Proverbs 14:12-13
  Luke 13:1-21

- **April 17**
  Joshua 23–24
  Psalm 47
  Proverbs 14:14
  Luke 13:22-35

- **April 18**
  Judges 1–2
  Psalm 48:1-7
  Proverbs 14:15-17
  Luke 14:1-24

- **April 19**
  Judges 3–4
  Psalm 48:8-14
  Proverbs 14:18-19
  Luke 14:25-35

- **April 20**
  Judges 5–6
  Psalm 49:1-9
  Proverbs 14:20-21
  Luke 15:1-10

- **April 21**
  Judges 7–8
  Psalm 49:10-20
  Proverbs 14:22-24
  Luke 15:11-32

- **April 22**
  Judges 9–10
  Psalm 50:1-6
  Proverbs 14:25-27
  Luke 16

- **April 23**
  Judges 11–12
  Psalm 50:7-15
  Proverbs 14:28
  Luke 17:1-19

- **April 24**
  Judges 13–14
  Psalm 50:16-23
  Proverbs 14:29-30
  Luke 17:20-37

- **April 25**
  Judges 15–16
  Psalm 51:1-5
  Proverbs 14:31-32
  Luke 18:1-25

- **April 26**
  Judges 17–19
  Psalm 51:6-9
  Proverbs 14:33-35
  Luke 18:26-43

- **April 27**
  Judges 20–21
  Psalm 51:10-19
  Proverbs 15:1-3
  Luke 19:1-27

- **April 28**
  Ruth 1–2
  Psalm 52:1-7
  Proverbs 15:4-5
  Luke 19:28-48

- **April 29**
  Ruth 3–4
  Psalm 52:8-9
  Proverbs 15:6-7
  Luke 20:1-26

- **April 30**
  1 Samuel 1–3
  Psalm 53
  Proverbs 15:8-11
  Luke 20:27-47

- **May 1**
  1 Samuel 4–5
  Psalm 54
  Proverbs 15:12-13
  Luke 21:1-19

- **May 2**
  1 Samuel 6–7
  Psalm 55:1-8
  Proverbs 15:14
  Luke 21:20-38

- **May 3**
  1 Samuel 8–9
  Psalm 55:9-14
  Proverbs 15:15-17
  Luke 22:1-23

- **May 4**
  1 Samuel 10–11
  Psalm 55:15-23
  Proverbs 15:18-20
  Luke 22:24-46

- **May 5**
  1 Samuel 12–13
  Psalm 56:1-13
  Proverbs 15:21-23
  Luke 22:47-71

- **May 6**
  1 Samuel 14–15
  Psalm 57:1-3
  Proverbs 15:24-25
  Luke 23:1-25

- **May 7**
  1 Samuel 16–17
  Psalm 57:4-11
  Proverbs 15:26
  Luke 23:26-56

- **May 8**
  1 Samuel 18–19
  Psalm 58
  Proverbs 15:27-30
  Luke 24:1-35

- **May 9**
  1 Samuel 20–21
  Psalm 59:1-5
  Proverbs 15:31-33
  Luke 24:36-53

- **May 10**
  1 Samuel 22–23
  Psalm 59:6-17
  Proverbs 16:1-2
  John 1:1-34

- **May 11**
  1 Samuel 24–25
  Psalm 60:1-5
  Proverbs 16:3
  John 1:35-51

- **May 12**
  1 Samuel 26–27
  Psalm 60:6-12
  Proverbs 16:4-5
  John 2

- **May 13**
  1 Samuel 28
  Psalm 61:1-3
  Proverbs 16:6
  John 3:1-21

- **May 14**
  1 Samuel 29–31
  Psalm 61:4-8
  Proverbs 16:7-9
  John 3:22-36

- **May 15**
  2 Samuel 1–2
  Psalm 62:1-4
  Proverbs 16:10-12
  John 4:1-42

- **May 16**
  2 Samuel 3-4
  Psalm 62:5-12
  Proverbs 16:13-15
  John 4:43-54

- **May 17**
  2 Samuel 5-6
  Psalm 63
  Proverbs 16:16-17
  John 5:1-18

- **May 18**
  2 Samuel 7-8
  Psalm 64
  Proverbs 16:18-19
  John 5:19-47

- **May 19**
  2 Samuel 9-10
  Psalm 65:1-8
  Proverbs 16:20-21
  John 6:1-21

- **May 20**
  2 Samuel 11-12
  Psalm 65:9-13
  Proverbs 16:22-24
  John 6:22-59

- **May 21**
  2 Samuel 13-14
  Psalm 66:1-7
  Proverbs 16:25-26
  John 6:60-71

- **May 22**
  2 Samuel 15-16
  Psalm 66:8-15
  Proverbs 16:27-30
  John 7:1-24

- **May 23**
  2 Samuel 17-18
  Psalm 66:16-20
  Proverbs 16:31-32
  John 7:25-53

- **May 24**
  2 Samuel 19-20
  Psalm 67
  Proverbs 16:33
  John 8:1-20

- **May 25**
  2 Samuel 21-22
  Psalm 68:1-6
  Proverbs 17:1-4
  John 8:21-59

- **May 26**
  2 Samuel 23-24
  Psalm 68:7-10
  Proverbs 17:5-6
  John 9:1-23

- **May 27**
  1 Kings 1-2
  Psalm 68:11-14
  Proverbs 17:7-9
  John 9:24-41

- **May 28**
  1 Kings 3-4
  Psalm 68:15-20
  Proverbs 17:10-12
  John 10:1-21

- **May 29**
  1 Kings 5-6
  Psalm 68:21-27
  Proverbs 17:13-15
  John 10:22-42

- **May 30**
  1 Kings 7-8
  Psalm 68:28-35
  Proverbs 17:16-17
  John 11:1-27

- **May 31**
  1 Kings 9-10
  Psalm 69:1-4
  Proverbs 17:18-19
  John 11:28-57

- **June 1**
  1 Kings 11-12
  Psalm 69:5-12
  Proverbs 17:20-22
  John 12:1-19

- **June 2**
  1 Kings 13-14
  Psalm 69:13-21
  Proverbs 17:23-24
  John 12:20-50

- **June 3**
  1 Kings 15–16
  Psalm 69:22–28
  Proverbs 17:25–26
  John 13:1–20

- **June 4**
  1 Kings 17–18
  Psalm 69:29–36
  Proverbs 17:27–28
  John 13:21–38

- **June 5**
  1 Kings 19–20
  Psalm 70:1–5
  Proverbs 18:1–2
  John 14

- **June 6**
  1 Kings 21–22
  Psalm 71:1–6
  Proverbs 18:3–5
  John 15

- **June 7**
  2 Kings 1–2
  Psalm 71:7–16
  Proverbs 18:6–8
  John 16

- **June 8**
  2 Kings 3–4
  Psalm 71:17–24
  Proverbs 18:9
  John 17

- **June 9**
  2 Kings 5–6
  Psalm 72:1–7
  Proverbs 18:10–11
  John 18:1–18

- **June 10**
  2 Kings 7–8
  Psalm 72:8–14
  Proverbs 18:12–13
  John 18:19–40

- **June 11**
  2 Kings 9–10
  Psalm 72:15–20
  Proverbs 18:14–15
  John 19:1–16

- **June 12**
  2 Kings 11–13
  Psalm 73:1–14
  Proverbs 18:16–17
  John 19:17–42

- **June 13**
  2 Kings 14
  Psalm 73:15–20
  Proverbs 18:18–19
  John 20

- **June 14**
  2 Kings 15–16
  Psalm 73:21–28
  Proverbs 18:20–21
  John 21

- **June 15**
  2 Kings 17–18
  Psalm 74:1–11
  Proverbs 18:22–24
  Acts 1

- **June 16**
  2 Kings 19–21
  Psalm 74:12–17
  Proverbs 19:1–2
  Acts 2:1–21

- **June 17**
  2 Kings 22–24
  Psalm 74:18–23
  Proverbs 19:3
  Acts 2:22–47

- **June 18**
  2 Kings 25
  Psalm 75
  Proverbs 19:4–5
  Acts 3

- **June 19**
  1 Chronicles 1–2
  Psalm 76:1–10
  Proverbs 19:6–7
  Acts 4:1–22

- **June 20**
  1 Chronicles 3–4
  Psalm 76:11–12
  Proverbs 19:8–9
  Acts 4:23–37

- **June 21**
  1 Chronicles 5-6
  Psalm 77:1-3
  Proverbs 19:10-12
  Acts 5:1-16

- **June 22**
  1 Chronicles 7-8
  Psalm 77:4-10
  Proverbs 19:13-14
  Acts 5:17-42

- **June 23**
  1 Chronicles 9-10
  Psalm 77:11-15
  Proverbs 19:15-16
  Acts 6

- **June 24**
  1 Chronicles 11-12
  Psalm 77:16-20
  Proverbs 19:17-19
  Acts 7:1-22

- **June 25**
  1 Chronicles 13-14
  Psalm 78:1-8
  Proverbs 19:20-21
  Acts 7:23-43

- **June 26**
  1 Chronicles 15-16
  Psalm 78:9-16
  Proverbs 19:22-24
  Acts 7:44-60

- **June 27**
  1 Chronicles 17-18
  Psalm 78:17-25
  Proverbs 19:25-26
  Acts 8:1-25

- **June 28**
  1 Chronicles 19-20
  Psalm 78:26-33
  Proverbs 19:27-29
  Acts 8:26-40

- **June 29**
  1 Chronicles 21-22
  Psalm 78:34-39
  Proverbs 20:1-2
  Acts 9:1-19

- **June 30**
  1 Chronicles 23-25
  Psalm 78:40-55
  Proverbs 20:3
  Acts 9:20-43

- **July 1**
  1 Chronicles 26-27
  Psalm 78:56-64
  Proverbs 20:4-5
  Acts 10:1-23

- **July 2**
  1 Chronicles 28-29
  Psalm 78:65-72
  Proverbs 20:6-7
  Acts 10:24-48

- **July 3**
  2 Chronicles 1-2
  Psalm 79:1-4
  Proverbs 20:8-9
  Acts 11

- **July 4**
  2 Chronicles 3-4
  Psalm 79:5-11
  Proverbs 20:10-12
  Acts 12

- **July 5**
  2 Chronicles 5-6
  Psalm 79:12-13
  Proverbs 20:13-14
  Acts 13:1-25

- **July 6**
  2 Chronicles 7-8
  Psalm 80:1-6
  Proverbs 20:15
  Acts 13:26-52

- **July 7**
  2 Chronicles 9-10
  Psalm 80:7-13
  Proverbs 20:16-18
  Acts 14

- **July 8**
  2 Chronicles 11-12
  Psalm 80:14-19
  Proverbs 20:19-21
  Acts 15:1-21

- **July 9**
  2 Chronicles 13-14
  Psalm 81:1-5
  Proverbs 20:22-23
  Acts 15:22-41

- **July 10**
  2 Chronicles 15-16
  Psalm 81:6-10
  Proverbs 20:24-25
  Acts 16:1-15

- **July 11**
  2 Chronicles 17-18
  Psalm 81:11-16
  Proverbs 20:26-28
  Acts 16:16-40

- **July 12**
  2 Chronicles 19-20
  Psalm 82
  Proverbs 20:29-30
  Acts 17:1-15

- **July 13**
  2 Chronicles 21-22
  Psalm 83:1-8
  Proverbs 21:1
  Acts 17:16-34

- **July 14**
  2 Chronicles 23-24
  Psalm 83:9-18
  Proverbs 21:2-3
  Acts 18

- **July 15**
  2 Chronicles 25-27
  Psalm 84:1-7
  Proverbs 21:4-5
  Acts 19:1-22

- **July 16**
  2 Chronicles 28-29
  Psalm 84:8-12
  Proverbs 21:6-8
  Acts 19:23-41

- **July 17**
  2 Chronicles 30-31
  Psalm 85:1-7
  Proverbs 21:9-11
  Acts 20:1-16

- **July 18**
  2 Chronicles 32-33
  Psalm 85:8-13
  Proverbs 21:12
  Acts 20:17-38

- **July 19**
  2 Chronicles 34-36
  Psalm 86:1-7
  Proverbs 21:13-14
  Acts 21:1-16

- **July 20**
  Ezra 1-2
  Psalm 86:8-13
  Proverbs 21:15-16
  Acts 21:17-40

- **July 21**
  Ezra 3-4
  Psalm 86:14-17
  Proverbs 21:17-18
  Acts 22

- **July 22**
  Ezra 5-6
  Psalm 87
  Proverbs 21:19-20
  Acts 23:1-22

- **July 23**
  Ezra 7-8
  Psalm 88:1-2
  Proverbs 21:21-22
  Acts 23:23-35

- **July 24**
  Ezra 9-10
  Psalm 88:3-10
  Proverbs 21:23-24
  Acts 24

- **July 25**
  Nehemiah 1-2
  Psalm 88:11-18
  Proverbs 21:25-26
  Acts 25

- **July 26**
  Nehemiah 3-5
  Psalm 89:1-4
  Proverbs 21:27
  Acts 26

- **July 27**
  Nehemiah 6-7
  Psalm 89:5-10
  Proverbs 21:28
  Acts 27:1-26

- **July 28**
  Nehemiah 8-9
  Psalm 89:11-18
  Proverbs 21:29-31
  Acts 27:27-44

- **July 29**
  Nehemiah 10-11
  Psalm 89:19-29
  Proverbs 22:1-2
  Acts 28

- **July 30**
  Nehemiah 12-13
  Psalm 89:30-37
  Proverbs 22:3-4
  Romans 1

- **July 31**
  Esther 1-2
  Psalm 89:38-45
  Proverbs 22:5-6
  Romans 2

- **August 1**
  Esther 3-4
  Psalm 89:46-52
  Proverbs 22:7-8
  Romans 3

- **August 2**
  Esther 5-6
  Psalm 90:1-6
  Proverbs 22:9
  Romans 4

- **August 3**
  Esther 7-8
  Psalm 90:7-17
  Proverbs 22:10-11
  Romans 5

- **August 4**
  Esther 9-10
  Psalm 91:1-8
  Proverbs 22:12
  Romans 6

- **August 5**
  Job 1-2
  Psalm 91:9-13
  Proverbs 22:13-14
  Romans 7

- **August 6**
  Job 3-4
  Psalm 91:14-16
  Proverbs 22:15
  Romans 8:1-17

- **August 7**
  Job 5-6
  Psalm 92:1-8
  Proverbs 22:16
  Romans 8:18-39

- **August 8**
  Job 7-8
  Psalm 92:9-15
  Proverbs 22:17-21
  Romans 9:1-18

- **August 9**
  Job 9-10
  Psalm 93
  Proverbs 22:22-23
  Romans 9:19-33

- **August 10**
  Job 11-12
  Psalm 94:1-11
  Proverbs 22:24-25
  Romans 10

- **August 11**
  Job 13-14
  Psalm 94:12-19
  Proverbs 22:26-27
  Romans 11:1-21

- **August 12**
  Job 15-16
  Psalm 94:20-23
  Proverbs 22:28-29
  Romans 11:22-36

- **August 13**
  Job 17-18
  Psalm 95:1-5
  Proverbs 23:1-3
  Romans 12

- **August 14**
  Job 19-20
  Psalm 95:6-11
  Proverbs 23:4-5
  Romans 13

- **August 15**
  Job 21-22
  Psalm 96:1-6
  Proverbs 23:6-8
  Romans 14

- **August 16**
  Job 23-24
  Psalm 96:7-10
  Proverbs 23:9
  Romans 15:1-13

- **August 17**
  Job 26
  Psalm 96:11-13
  Proverbs 23:10-12
  Romans 15:14-33

- **August 18**
  Job 27-28
  Psalm 97:1-6
  Proverbs 23:13-14
  Romans 16

- **August 19**
  Job 29-30
  Psalm 97:7-12
  Proverbs 23:15-16
  1 Corinthians 1

- **August 20**
  Job 31-32
  Psalm 98:1-3
  Proverbs 23:17-18
  1 Corinthians 2

- **August 21**
  Job 33-34
  Psalm 98:4-9
  Proverbs 23:19-21
  1 Corinthians 3

- **August 22**
  Job 35-36
  Psalm 99
  Proverbs 23:22-25
  1 Corinthians 4

- **August 23**
  Job 37-38
  Psalm 100
  Proverbs 23:26-28
  1 Corinthians 5

- **August 24**
  Job 39-40
  Psalm 101:1-4
  Proverbs 23:29-30
  1 Corinthians 6

- **August 25**
  Job 41-42
  Psalm 101:5-8
  Proverbs 23:31-35
  1 Corinthians 7:1-16

- **August 26**
  Ecclesiastes 1-2
  Psalm 102:1-11
  Proverbs 24:1-2
  1 Corinthians 7:17-40

- **August 27**
  Ecclesiastes 3
  Psalm 102:12-17
  Proverbs 24:3-4
  1 Corinthians 8

- **August 28**
  Ecclesiastes 4-6
  Psalm 102:18-28
  Proverbs 24:5-6
  1 Corinthians 9

- **August 29**
  Ecclesiastes 7
  Psalm 103:1-5
  Proverbs 24:7-9
  1 Corinthians 10:1-22

- **August 30**
  Ecclesiastes 8-10
  Psalm 103:6-14
  Proverbs 24:10-12
  1 Corinthians 10:23-33

- **August 31**
  Ecclesiastes 11-12
  Psalm 103:15-22
  Proverbs 24:13-14
  1 Corinthians 11:1-16

- **September 1**
  Song of Songs 1-2
  Psalm 104:1-9
  Proverbs 24:15-16
  1 Corinthians 11:17-34

- **September 2**
  Song of Songs 3-4
  Psalm 104:10-23
  Proverbs 24:17-18
  1 Corinthians 12

- **September 3**
  Song of Songs 5-6
  Psalm 104:24-30
  Proverbs 24:19-20
  1 Corinthians 13

- **September 4**
  Song of Songs 7-8
  Psalm 104:31-35
  Proverbs 24:21-22
  1 Corinthians 14:1-25

- **September 5**
  Isaiah 1-2
  Psalm 105:1-7
  Proverbs 24:23-25
  1 Corinthians 14:26-40

- **September 6**
  Isaiah 3-4
  Psalm 105:8-15
  Proverbs 24:26-27
  1 Corinthians 15:1-34

- **September 7**
  Isaiah 5-6
  Psalm 105:16-36
  Proverbs 24:28-29
  1 Corinthians 15:35-58

- **September 8**
  Isaiah 7-8
  Psalm 105:37-45
  Proverbs 24:30-34
  1 Corinthians 16:1-24

- **September 9**
  Isaiah 9-10
  Psalm 106:1-5
  Proverbs 25:1-2
  2 Corinthians 1

- **September 10**
  Isaiah 11-12
  Psalm 106:6-18
  Proverbs 25:3-5
  2 Corinthians 2

- **September 11**
  Isaiah 13-14
  Psalm 106:19-23
  Proverbs 25:6-8
  2 Corinthians 3

- **September 12**
  Isaiah 15-16
  Psalm 106:24-31
  Proverbs 25:9-10
  2 Corinthians 4:1-15

- **September 13**
  Isaiah 17-18
  Psalm 106:32-39
  Proverbs 25:11-12
  2 Corinthians 4:16-5:21

- **September 14**
  Isaiah 19-20
  Psalm 106:40-48
  Proverbs 25:13
  2 Corinthians 6

- **September 15**
  Isaiah 21-22
  Psalm 107:1-9
  Proverbs 25:14-15
  2 Corinthians 7

- **September 16**
  Isaiah 23-24
  Psalm 107:10-22
  Proverbs 25:16-17
  2 Corinthians 8

- **September 17**
  Isaiah 25-26
  Psalm 107:23-32
  Proverbs 25:18-19
  2 Corinthians 9

- **September 18**
  Isaiah 27-28
  Psalm 107:33-43
  Proverbs 25:20
  2 Corinthians 10

- **September 19**
  Isaiah 29
  Psalm 108:1-5
  Proverbs 25:21-22
  2 Corinthians 11:1-15

- **September 20**
  Isaiah 30-32
  Psalm 108:6-13
  Proverbs 25:23-24
  2 Corinthians 11:16-33

- **September 21**
  Isaiah 33-34
  Psalm 109:1-5
  Proverbs 25:25-26
  2 Corinthians 12

- **September 22**
  Isaiah 35-36
  Psalm 109:6-15
  Proverbs 25:27-28
  2 Corinthians 13

- **September 23**
  Isaiah 37-38
  Psalm 109:16-20
  Proverbs 26:1
  Galatians 1

- **September 24**
  Isaiah 39-40
  Psalm 109:21-25
  Proverbs 26:2
  Galatians 2

- **September 25**
  Isaiah 41-42
  Psalm 109:26-31
  Proverbs 26:3-4
  Galatians 3

- **September 26**
  Isaiah 43-44
  Psalm 110
  Proverbs 26:5-9
  Galatians 4

- **September 27**
  Isaiah 45-46
  Psalm 111
  Proverbs 26:10
  Galatians 5

- **September 28**
  Isaiah 47-48
  Psalm 111:7-10
  Proverbs 26:11-12
  Galatians 6

- **September 29**
  Isaiah 49-50
  Psalm 112:1-4
  Proverbs 26:13-15
  Ephesians 1

- **September 30**
  Isaiah 51-52
  Psalm 112:5-10
  Proverbs 26:16
  Ephesians 2

- **October 1**
  Isaiah 53-54
  Psalm 113:1-4
  Proverbs 26:17-19
  Ephesians 3

- **October 2**
  Isaiah 55-56
  Psalm 113:5-9
  Proverbs 26:20-21
  Ephesians 4

- **October 3**
  Isaiah 57-58
  Psalm 114
  Proverbs 26:22
  Ephesians 5:1-20

- **October 4**
  Isaiah 59-60
  Psalm 115:1-8
  Proverbs 26:23
  Ephesians 5:21-33

- **October 5**
  Isaiah 61-62
  Psalm 115:9-13
  Proverbs 26:24-26
  Ephesians 6

- **October 6**
  Isaiah 63-64
  Psalm 115:14-18
  Proverbs 26:27
  Philippians 1

- **October 7**
  Isaiah 65-66
  Psalm 116:1-4
  Proverbs 26:28
  Philippians 2

- **October 8**
  Jeremiah 1-2
  Psalm 116:5-14
  Proverbs 27:1
  Philippians 3

- **October 9**
  Jeremiah 3-4
  Psalm 116:15-19
  Proverbs 27:2
  Philippians 4

- **October 10**
  Jeremiah 5-6
  Psalm 117
  Proverbs 27:3-4
  Colossians 1

- **October 11**
  Jeremiah 7-8
  Psalm 118:1-4
  Proverbs 27:5-6
  Colossians 2

- **October 12**
  Jeremiah 9-10
  Psalm 118:5-9
  Proverbs 27:7
  Colossians 3

- **October 13**
  Jeremiah 11-12
  Psalm 118:10-14
  Proverbs 27:8
  Colossians 4

- **October 14**
  Jeremiah 13-14
  Psalm 118:15-21
  Proverbs 27:9
  1 Thessalonians 1

- **October 15**
  Jeremiah 15-16
  Psalm 118:22-24
  Proverbs 27:10
  1 Thessalonians 2

- **October 16**
  Jeremiah 17-18
  Psalm 118:25-29
  Proverbs 27:11-12
  1 Thessalonians 3

- **October 17**
  Jeremiah 19-20
  Psalm 119:1-8
  Proverbs 27:13
  1 Thessalonians 4

- **October 18**
  Jeremiah 21-22
  Psalm 119:9-16
  Proverbs 27:14
  1 Thessalonians 5

- **October 19**
  Jeremiah 23-24
  Psalm 119:17-24
  Proverbs 27:15-16
  2 Thessalonians 1

- **October 20**
  Jeremiah 25-26
  Psalm 119:25-32
  Proverbs 27:17
  2 Thessalonians 2

- **October 21**
  Jeremiah 27-28
  Psalm 119:33-40
  Proverbs 27:18
  2 Thessalonians 3

- **October 22**
  Jeremiah 29-30
  Psalm 119:41-48
  Proverbs 27:19
  1 Timothy 1

- **October 23**
  Jeremiah 31-32
  Psalm 119:49-56
  Proverbs 27:20
  1 Timothy 2

- **October 24**
  Jeremiah 33-34
  Psalm 119:57-64
  Proverbs 27:21
  1 Timothy 3

- **October 25**
  Jeremiah 35–36
  Psalm 119:65-72
  Proverbs 27:22
  1 Timothy 4

- **October 26**
  Jeremiah 37–38
  Psalm 119:73-80
  Proverbs 27:23-27
  1 Timothy 5

- **October 27**
  Jeremiah 39–40
  Psalm 119:81-88
  Proverbs 28:1
  1 Timothy 6

- **October 28**
  Jeremiah 41–42
  Psalm 119:89-96
  Proverbs 28:2
  2 Timothy 1

- **October 29**
  Jeremiah 43–44
  Psalm 119:97-104
  Proverbs 28:3
  2 Timothy 2

- **October 30**
  Jeremiah 45–46
  Psalm 119:105-112
  Proverbs 28:4
  2 Timothy 3

- **October 31**
  Jeremiah 47–48
  Psalm 119:113-120
  Proverbs 28:5
  2 Timothy 4

- **November 1**
  Jeremiah 49–50
  Psalm 119:121-128
  Proverbs 28:6
  Titus 1

- **November 2**
  Jeremiah 51–52
  Psalm 119:129-136
  Proverbs 28:7-8
  Titus 2

- **November 3**
  Lamentations 1–2
  Psalm 119:137-144
  Proverbs 28:9-10
  Titus 3

- **November 4**
  Lamentations 3–5
  Psalm 119:145-152
  Proverbs 28:11
  Philemon 1–25

- **November 5**
  Ezekiel 1–2
  Psalm 119:153-160
  Proverbs 28:12
  Hebrews 1:1-14

- **November 6**
  Ezekiel 3–4
  Psalm 119:161-168
  Proverbs 28:13
  Hebrews 2

- **November 7**
  Ezekiel 5–6
  Psalm 119:169-176
  Proverbs 28:14
  Hebrews 3

- **November 8**
  Ezekiel 7–8
  Psalm 120
  Proverbs 28:15
  Hebrews 4

- **November 9**
  Ezekiel 9–10
  Psalm 121
  Proverbs 28:16
  Hebrews 5

- **November 10**
  Ezekiel 11–12
  Psalm 122:1-5
  Proverbs 28:17-18
  Hebrews 6

- **November 11**
  Ezekiel 13–14
  Psalm 122:6-9
  Proverbs 28:19
  Hebrews 7

- **November 12**
  Ezekiel 15-16
  Psalm 123
  Proverbs 28:20
  Hebrews 8

- **November 13**
  Ezekiel 17-18
  Psalm 124
  Proverbs 28:21
  Hebrews 9

- **November 14**
  Ezekiel 19-20
  Psalm 125
  Proverbs 28:22
  Hebrews 10:1-18

- **November 15**
  Ezekiel 21-22
  Psalm 126
  Proverbs 28:23
  Hebrews 10:19-39

- **November 16**
  Ezekiel 23-24
  Psalm 127
  Proverbs 28:24
  Hebrews 11:1-16

- **November 17**
  Ezekiel 25-26
  Psalm 128
  Proverbs 28:25
  Hebrews 11:17-40

- **November 18**
  Ezekiel 27-28
  Psalm 129:1-4
  Proverbs 28:26
  Hebrews 12

- **November 19**
  Ezekiel 29-30
  Psalm 129:5-8
  Proverbs 28:27
  Hebrews 13

- **November 20**
  Ezekiel 31-32
  Psalm 130:1-4
  Proverbs 28:28
  James 1

- **November 21**
  Ezekiel 33-34
  Psalm 130:5-8
  Proverbs 29:1
  James 2

- **November 22**
  Ezekiel 35-36
  Psalm 131
  Proverbs 29:2-3
  James 3

- **November 23**
  Ezekiel 37-38
  Psalm 132:1-9
  Proverbs 29:4
  James 4

- **November 24**
  Ezekiel 39-40
  Psalm 132:10-18
  Proverbs 29:5
  James 5

- **November 25**
  Ezekiel 41-42
  Psalm 133
  Proverbs 29:6
  1 Peter 1

- **November 26**
  Ezekiel 43-44
  Psalm 134
  Proverbs 29:7
  1 Peter 2

- **November 27**
  Ezekiel 45-46
  Psalm 135:1-7
  Proverbs 29:8
  1 Peter 3

- **November 28**
  Ezekiel 47-48
  Psalm 135:8-14
  Proverbs 29:9
  1 Peter 4

- **November 29**
  Daniel 1-2
  Psalm 135:15-21
  Proverbs 29:10
  1 Peter 5

- **November 30**
  Daniel 3-4
  Psalm 136:1-9
  Proverbs 29:11
  2 Peter 1

- **December 1**
  Daniel 5-6
  Psalm 136:10-26
  Proverbs 29:12-13
  2 Peter 2

- **December 2**
  Daniel 7-8
  Psalm 137:1-6
  Proverbs 29:14
  2 Peter 3

- **December 3**
  Daniel 9-10
  Psalm 137:7-9
  Proverbs 29:15
  1 John 1

- **December 4**
  Daniel 11-12
  Psalm 138:1-3
  Proverbs 29:16
  1 John 2

- **December 5**
  Hosea 1-2
  Psalm 138:4-5
  Proverbs 29:17
  1 John 3

- **December 6**
  Hosea 3-4
  Psalm 138:6-8
  Proverbs 29:18
  1 John 4

- **December 7**
  Hosea 5-6
  Psalm 139:1-6
  Proverbs 29:19
  1 John 5

- **December 8**
  Hosea 7-8
  Psalm 139:7-12
  Proverbs 29:20
  2 John 1-13

- **December 9**
  Hosea 9-10
  Psalm 139:13-16
  Proverbs 29:21
  3 John 1-15

- **December 10**
  Hosea 11-12
  Psalm 139:17-24
  Proverbs 29:22
  Jude 1-25

- **December 11**
  Hosea 13-14
  Psalm 140:1-5
  Proverbs 29:23
  Revelation 1

- **December 12**
  Joel 1-3
  Psalm 140:6-13
  Proverbs 29:24
  Revelation 2

- **December 13**
  Amos 1-3
  Psalm 141:1-4
  Proverbs 29:25
  Revelation 3

- **December 14**
  Amos 4-5
  Psalm 141:5-10
  Proverbs 29:26
  Revelation 4

- **December 15**
  Amos 6-7
  Psalm 142:1-7
  Proverbs 29:27
  Revelation 5

- **December 16**
  Amos 8-9
  Psalm 143:1-6
  Proverbs 30:1-4
  Revelation 6

- **December 17**
  Obadiah 1-21
  Psalm 143:7-12
  Proverbs 30:5-6
  Revelation 7

- **December 18**
  Jonah 1-4
  Psalm 144:1-8
  Proverbs 30:7-9
  Revelation 8

- **December 19**
  Micah 1-3
  Psalm 144:9-15
  Proverbs 30:10
  Revelation 9

- **December 20**
  Micah 4-5
  Psalm 145:1-7
  Proverbs 30:11-12
  Revelation 10

- **December 21**
  Micah 6-7
  Psalm 145:8-16
  Proverbs 30:13-14
  Revelation 11

- **December 22**
  Nahum 1-3
  Psalm 145:17-21
  Proverbs 30:15-16
  Revelation 12

- **December 23**
  Habakkuk 1-3
  Psalm 146:1-10
  Proverbs 30:17
  Revelation 13

- **December 24**
  Zephaniah 1-3
  Psalm 147:1-6
  Proverbs 30:18-19
  Revelation 14

- **December 25**
  Haggai 1-2
  Psalm 147:7-11
  Proverbs 30:20
  Revelation 15

- **December 26**
  Zechariah 1-3
  Psalm 147:12-20
  Proverbs 30:21-23
  Revelation 16

- **December 27**
  Zechariah 4-6
  Psalm 148:1-6
  Proverbs 30:24-28
  Revelation 17

- **December 28**
  Zechariah 7-9
  Psalm 148:7-14
  Proverbs 30:29-31
  Revelation 18

- **December 29**
  Zechariah 10-12
  Psalm 149:1-5
  Proverbs 30:32-33
  Revelation 19

- **December 30**
  Zechariah 12-14
  Psalm 149:6-9
  Proverbs 31:1-9
  Revelation 20

- **December 31**
  Malachi 1-4
  Psalm 150
  Proverbs 31:10-31
  Revelation 21-22

THE 15-MINUTE BREAKTHROUGH

By Robert Morris

If I told you that you could experience miracles by doing something for 15 minutes a day, would you do it? I am talking about having a daily quiet time. You might cringe when you hear that phrase because so many of us have had bad experiences in this area. We have tried to have a quiet time, but it wasn't very good. When we hear other people talking about their quiet times, it seems like Moses, Elijah, and Jesus show up—but some of us simply don't have quiet times like that. We might even fall asleep during our quiet times. And eventually, we just give up on the whole idea. We think, "I'm a Christian. I love God. I serve God and come to church, but I'm just never going to have a quiet time like other people."

I used to feel that way too, so I want to help you by disproving *three common myths* about quiet times.

1. You can only have a quiet time from 4 to 6 am.

I used to travel and preach at crusades and revivals. Our services started at 7 pm every evening, and most nights I didn't get to bed until midnight or later. For years, I was a late riser. But when I would get around my friends in ministry who were early risers, they always talked about how they met with God at 5 am. It sounded so spiritual, and it made me feel terrible because I didn't get up early to have a quiet time.

I want you to understand this: If you show up later than 7 am, God isn't going to say, "Sorry, we're closed. You should have come earlier when the spiritual people were here." You can have a quiet time whatever time of day you want. I suggest doing it at the start of your day, but it's important to realize you can have it anytime.

2. Your quiet time must last at least one hour.

There is nothing in the Bible about a one-hour-minimum requirement for spending time with God. I know there are those who think that "spiritual" people need to spend at least an hour each day having a quiet time, but I'm a pastor, and I don't do that. The reason why is I am a bottom-line kind of person. I'm not a long-winded preacher. I like to get to the bottom line, and my prayers are that way too.

3. Your prayer journal must sound like the Bible.

Have you ever had someone read to you from their prayer journal, and it was unbelievably awesome? I was with a group of ministers once when one of the guys said, "I want to read something to you that the Lord spoke to me this past Tuesday." As he read, I thought, "I have *never* heard anything like that in my life." There was such poetry to it! Wondering what God spoke to me on that Tuesday, I looked in my journal, and this is what I had written: "Try not to be a jerk today." That is what the Lord had spoken to me! It wasn't eloquent or poetic. But it was real.

God doesn't want to burden you with "rules" about quiet times that other people have set. He just wants to spend time with you. Can you imagine what it would be like to have to go down a checklist when we are trying to spend time with God?

Now that we have cleared the air, I want to show you four things that have helped me tremendously in my quiet time. I absolutely believe 15 minutes with the Lord each day can change your life.

Quiet Your Mind

Let all that I am wait quietly before God, for my hope is in him (Psalm 62:5).

In this passage, David tells his soul to be quiet before God, and we need to do the same. A quiet time is not a time to be busy; it's a time to slow down. In order to do that, you are going to have to quiet your mind and soul.

Focus Your Mind on God

Shout with joy to the Lord, all the earth! Worship the Lord with gladness. Come before him, singing with joy. Acknowledge that the Lord is God! He made us, and we are his. We are his people, the sheep of his pasture. Enter his gates with thanksgiving; go into his courts with praise. Give thanks to him and praise his name. For the Lord is good. His unfailing love continues forever, and his faithfulness continues to each generation (Psalm 100).

When I go to meet with the Lord and quiet my mind, God always puts a song in my heart. For the rest of the day, that song is my key into God's presence. If you will just listen, He will give you a song too. You can sing it out loud if you want to, but you don't have to. What is important is that you are focusing on Him. Singing to the Lord turns your focus toward God, and it can be your key into His presence.

Pray What's on Your Mind

Don't worry about anything; instead, pray about everything. Tell God what you need, and thank him for all he has done (Philippians 4:6).

Just talk to God like you talk to anyone else, and pray about whatever concerns you. You don't have to pray for world peace unless that is on your heart. Pray about what is burdening you. You are never going to pray passionately until you pray about something you are burdened about. You can pray for your kids, your marriage, your job, or your finances. It doesn't matter. Simply pray about whatever God has put on your heart and mind.

Renew Your Mind

Don't copy the behavior and customs of this world, but let God transform you into a new person by changing the way you think. Then you will learn to know God's will for you, which is good and pleasing and perfect (Romans 12:2).

Renewing your mind will transform every area of your life, and the process is simple: Read God's Word every day. There have been so many times when something I read in the morning was exactly what I needed for that day. God's Word gives me life, peace, and strength. It's like lifting weights—sometimes it feels good, and sometimes it doesn't. But if you persevere and do it consistently, you are going to see results over time. The more regularly you read the Bible, the stronger you will become spiritually. Reading God's Word every day renews your mind, changes your thinking, and transforms you into His image!

On September 16, 1999, I had my quiet time like any other day, but something special happened as I met with God. After I prayed, I asked the Lord, "Where do You want me to read?" Very clearly, I heard God say, "Genesis 35 and Deuteronomy 11." So I opened up to Genesis 35 and read, "Move to Bethel and build an altar for Me there" (v. 1 paraphrase). As soon as I read that, the Holy Spirit immediately spoke to me and said, "Move to Southlake and start a church." As I kept reading, God began unfolding His plan for Gateway Church. Where Gateway is today all came out of that little quiet time several years ago!

What is five years down the road for you? What is ten years down the road? God knows. Are you giving Him an opportunity to tell you? Please don't miss it because you are too busy. All it takes is 15 minutes.

MEMORY VERSES

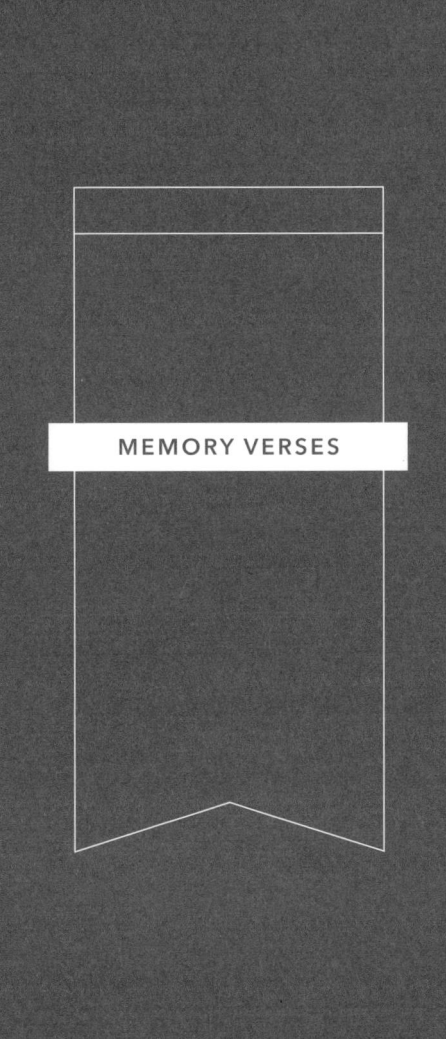

1

"You are the light of the world—like a city on a hilltop that cannot be hidden. No one lights a lamp and then puts it under a basket. Instead, a lamp is placed on a stand, where it gives light to everyone in the house. In the same way, let your good deeds shine out for all to see, so that everyone will praise your heavenly Father."

Matthew 5:14-16

2

"Keep on asking, and you will receive what you ask for. Keep on seeking, and you will find. Keep on knocking, and the door will be opened to you. For everyone who asks, receives. Everyone who seeks, finds. And to everyone who knocks, the door will be opened."

Matthew 7:7-8

3

"Come to me, all of you who are weary and carry heavy burdens, and I will give you rest. Take my yoke upon you. Let me teach you, because I am humble and gentle at heart, and you will find rest for your souls. For my yoke is easy to bear, and the burden I give you is light."

Matthew 11:28-30